I THOUGHT IT WAS AN ABSOLUTE CONTRADICTION: God's Ways Versus Our Ways

Margaret A. Donaldson Cobb

Foreword by Rev. Anita Michelle Cobb

Margaret A. Donaldson Cobb

Enhanced DNA Publishing
www.EnhancedDNAPublishing.com
info@EnhancedDNA1.com
317-537-1438

I THOUGHT IT WAS AN ABSOLUTE CONTRADICTION:
God's Ways Versus Our Ways
Copyright © 2023 Margaret A. Donaldson Cobb
Cover by Anthony Cobb
Photography by Charles Donnell Photography

All rights reserved.
No portion of this publication may be reproduced, stored in any electronic system, or transmitted in any form or by any means without the written permission from the author. Brief quotations may be used in literary reviews.

Unless otherwise noted, all Scripture quotations are used from the King James Version of the Bible.

ISBN-13: 979-8-9874187-6-5

I Thought it was An Absolute Contradiction

Margaret A. Donaldson Cobb

GOD

Beloved, I wish above all things that thou mayest prosper and be in health, even as thy soul prosper. 3 John verse 2

DEDICATION

This book is dedicated to my mother Anita Louise Hogue Donaldson. Woman of God. Woman of resilience. I am because of her. The A. in my name is Anita. We are mother and daughter and also each other's confidant. I am her legacy, as well as my daughter and line sister Anita Michelle, my sister Pamela and another granddaughter Cherinee of Alpha Kappa Alpha Sorority Inc. Mom continues at 86 to play the piano for churches. Mom had a wonderful marriage of 63 years to my father, William Hiram Donaldson, I who passed in 2020. Together they had the three of us, awesome parents to my big brother William II and little sister Pamela Donaldson Johnson. Mom has seven grandchildren, and six great grandchildren. Life has changed but her faith and trust in God remains the same.

Dedicating also to my children Andrew II, Tracey, Anthony and Anita Michelle. Along with my grandchildren Andrea Simone, Alyssa Sanaa, Andrew III (Drew).

And to all those who think trusting God is An Absolute Contradiction.

Margaret A. Donaldson Cobb

ACKNOWLEDGMENTS

To those who are never acknowledged:

The left behind
The left out
The left alone
The lied on
The least
The last
The lost
The un-liked
The locked up
and
The locked out

Contrary to what one would believe I have been all of the above. Left behind while watching others go forward. Left out when others did not want me to be with them. Left alone on days when I needed you the most. Lied on. The least of those who **seemed** to have the most, but they really had less than I did. The last one in line. Lost when I could not find my way. Not liked and sometimes for no reason. Lock up like a caged bird desiring to open the door and fly. Locked out and did not know I had the key to unlock the door. And sometimes I thought I was An Absolute Contradiction.

Margaret A. Donaldson Cobb

In loving memory of my dad! My first heartbeat:

William Hiram Donaldson, I
7-10-1934 to 6-6-20

In loving memory of my beloved husband:

Andrew Cobb, I
11-27-58 to 10-13-2016

Established as one: 10-27-1979
Death did us part: 10-13-2016

TABLE OF CONTENTS

DEDICATION 5
ACKNOWLEDGMENTS 7
FOREWORD 11
INTRODUCTION 15
CHAPTER 1: LOVE YOUR ENEMIES 17
CHAPTER 2: JOY IN THE MIDST OF SORROW 23
CHAPTER 3: GIVE TO RECEIVE 31
CHAPTER 4: FROM THE GUTTERMOST TO THE UTTERMOST 39
CHAPTER 5: FINE DECEPTION 47
CHAPTER 6: THE FOOLISHNESS OF PREACHING 55
CHAPTER 7: NO WAY OUT BUT BY ME 65
CHAPTER 8: LOVE BEARS ALL 73
CHAPTER 9: THE LEAST OF THEM HAD THE MOST 81
CHAPTER 10: A CHILD CAN LEAD 89
CHAPTER 11: SEARCH FOR THE LIGHT IN THE DARK AND LISTEN FOR GOD IN THE MIDST OF THE NOISE 97
CHAPTER 12: STANDING ON SHAKY GROUND 107
CHAPTER 13: A WAY THAT SEEMS RIGHT 113
CHAPTER 14: FORFEITED PEACE/NEEDLESS PAIN 121
CHAPTER 15: I THOUGHT IT WAS AN ABSOLUTE CONTRADICTION ... 129
ABOUT THE AUTHOR 135

Margaret A. Donaldson Cobb

FOREWORD

When we think of what the world says and does and compare it to the word of God there are often many things that do not line up. There are ideas and concepts that do not make sense. How do we begin to make them make sense in the world we live in today? How do we begin to understand that what we are reading are not actually contradictions but models of ways to live. Before we continue into this work, we must understand the words being used. Absolute and Contradiction According to Oxford's Languages Dictionary, the *word* **absolute** *means a value or principle that is regarded as universally valid, or which may be viewed without relation to other things.* See also, definite, sure confirmed. While a **contradiction** *is a combination of statements, ideas, or features of a situation that are opposed to one another.* Understanding these two words sets the stage for understanding that the ideas that are presented are absolute contradictions to the ways of the world, but are the guiding principles to the way of God.

Jesus spoke in parables to help the disciples learn hard complicated concepts. They did not always get it even after Jesus explained it to them. Jesus did not stop making sure they were prepared to face the world that would be very different from what he was teaching. Love thy enemy. Turn the other cheek. Let the Children come. Wild ideas that the people of the time and even today still have trouble processing.

In "I Thought it was an Absolute Contradiction", we have an opportunity to see hard concepts from a different light. This book takes the personal story of author Margaret D. Cobb and weaves it into biblical truths. This book highlights insights learned throughout the years and testifies to the Goodness of God. I Thought it was An Absolute Contradiction takes the familiar passages of scriptures and helps the reader to have a clearer understanding of what is being said. It provides an opportunity for the common reader to find themselves on the journey to realize what they thought were contradictions were really opportunities to see God's handiwork.

In life we are consumed by what society says and does. We as a people want to please those in authority over us not realizing how the compromises that are made to feed another person's ego may stunt our growth and knowledge. We become contradictions of who we say we are. This book helps to remind us of who we are and how we got there. Yes, this book is for the believer, however, anyone who takes the time to read, to learn, to hear, will find themselves asking the hard questions.

This author has lived and is living with the revelation of the contradictions she writes about. In 1979 a young, newlywed, soon to be mother was cast aside. There was no way she would be able to overcome the obstacles that would surely face her. This young, newlywed, soon to be mother would go on to have two more children, endure the pressures of struggles, a spouse with health challenges, moving homes what felt like every year for several years, losing herself and almost her marriage to raising three college educated children, restoring a marriage, finishing college at the master's level herself, and more. Her very life is a contradiction to what society had deemed her path. She was able to push through and persevere because of her faith in God and standing on the promises that God made to her. She leaned into the contradictions and is living a life that says, "if God be for me who can be against me." Her children are the balanced products of their environments. God fearing, law abiding, self-sufficient adults. Their story could have gone either way. Her sons could be in jail, on drugs, deadbeats. Her daughter could have multiple children, promiscuous ways, and very low self-esteem. That was the trajectory laid out before them and yet they followed a different path. Their lives are contradictory to the plan society had deemed to be their portion. Now, her children are grown, and they are not perfect. They have had to overcome obstacles in their own ways, but they continue to choose what to the world is a contradiction. They continue to love when love seems evasive. They continue to help when it doesn't always feel reciprocated. They continue to choose Christ because he has never failed them yet.

May you read this book with an open mind and heart. May you see yourself, your family, your friends on the pages and be encouraged. What you will learn is that the word of God is not a contradiction of itself, but it is vastly different from the way of the world, and it yields a better harvest. Hard days come and going with the flow is easy, but trust in the Lord with all your heart and lean not into your own understanding (Proverbs 3:5 paraphrased).

Rev. Anita M. Cobb, Daughter.

Margaret A. Donaldson Cobb

INTRODUCTION

"*This is a contradiction!! An absolute contradiction!!*" was my reaction and response to John 16:33. I could not understand how in my trials God would say "...In this world you shall have tribulations" and in the same breath told me to "be of good cheer". I responded the same way to James 1:3, counting "all" things as joy. All includes the bad. What I realized was though it sounds like **An Absolute Contradiction**, it was and is words to live by that strengthens our faith, gives us hope where we cannot see hope.

My desire for **"I Thought it was An Absolute Contradiction"** is that it will speak life to you when you feel you can't go on. When some things hurt so bad, and some things are just too hard to comprehend. **I Thought it was An Absolute Contradiction** will witness to the depth of your soul and causes the peace that passes all understanding to reign on your life.

I am a witness writer. The ministry of the written word can be an effectual tool that will assist in walking the narrow path home to glory. For when it is written to the glory of God and from God then the word will be a light unto our feet and a lamp on our journey.

I know I look at life with rose-colored glasses. I have seen enough of life's heartaches, fears, trials through the dark lens of life that even on a well-written television show, I don't want to see it. I know there is someone whose lens is thicker and darker than the ones I look through; but that is their or your story to tell. My story is to witness or testify to the glory of God, that nothing – no-thing is too hard for God.

I Thought it was An Absolute Contradiction is the ultimate "versus" battle, God's way versus our way. (Who you with?) Proverbs 14:12 says, "A way that seems right by man will lead to his (or her) destruction. This scripture is from the Old Testament. The law, the Old Testament still applies. Despite the debate about the Old Testament, it is so relevant today and the New Testament bears witness to it with grace. Being under grace was God's way of loving us and released us from the activity of slaughtering animals for our sins; that Jesus was sacrificed as animals were in the Old Testament. The difference was the choice and the reason. By crucifixion God allowed his Son to be sacrificed for the remission of sin that He knew we would commit. The choice was Jesus accepting crucifixion knowing how we would act. Now, the reason He accepted dying by the way of the cross for our sins was love. Christ atoned for our sins that we would be at-one with God. I ask again, "who you with"?

I Thought it was An Absolute Contradiction will in no way contradict the word of God. The witness in this book will go forth in a way that will cause examination and not judgement. It will be simple but profound. Encouraging and inspirational. Prayerfully enjoyed by all who will read it. Unfortunately, those who may really need this book may never read it; but you will and if ever you get the chance to share it let him or her know that the sacrifice and love of God is not An Absolute Contradiction.

CHAPTER 1: LOVE YOUR ENEMIES

The thought of praying for an enemy is contrary to the way of the world and the way I used to think. There was a time when I felt as though I thought you were my enemy, I would not even call your name nevertheless pray for you.

The enemy stole from me.
    Love your enemy.
The enemy hurt my child.
    Love your enemy.
The enemy killed my loved ones.
    Love your enemy.
The enemy destroyed my life.
    Love your enemy.
The enemy caused me to lose my job.
    Love your enemy.
The enemy caused me to lose my marriage.
    Love your enemy.
The enemy caused me to lose my best friend.
    Love your enemy.
The enemy caused me to be deceived.
    Love your enemy.
The enemy presented itself to me and I almost lost my soul.
    Love your enemy.
The list can go on and on about what the enemy may try and do but, there is only one remedy, antidote, or solution in winning this war, is with prayer. My first reaction to

whatever the enemy's plan of attack would be, was contradictory, loving or praying first. The more I learn about God, I realize I would never be able to forgive without loving or praying to God first.

In dealing with an enemy or enemies loving/praying, and forgiveness goes together. Once you can love you can also pray for an enemy; you are able to forgive them as well. It may be contradictory to love or pray for someone and not forgive them. The question you may ask is, which one comes first? At this point it really does not matter; forgive and love or pray and forgive. Either way you are being obedient to God, liberating yourself and going on with your life.

Sometimes I would have to pray for myself to be able to love and pray for my enemies. Even though I am growing spiritually more and more every day, even though I pray daily, even though I asked for forgiveness daily and expect to be forgiven, depending on the level of the attack from my enemy I would still need much time with God to get to that point. I have experienced an instant reaction of forgiveness and I have also experienced a reaction from not forgiving. There have been times when I thought that I had forgiven a person and realized that truly in my heart I had not.

You can always tell if you have truly forgiven someone or not. If you say you have prayed and forgiven someone and when you see them, that old feeling creeps up with a silent attitude, then in your heart, forgiveness has **not** taken place. You know you have successfully prayed and forgiven someone when that does not happen, and you can treat them as you did before the attack. I pray that as a Christian, a true believer and follower of Christ that I would not have a second thought, that I would be able to pray for my enemies immediately. That takes a real mature Christian.

We always want to know "what would Jesus do?"
But I (Jesus) say unto you love your enemies. (Matthew 5:44 a) How to love your enemies? By using Jesus Christ as an example. He was crucified by his enemies, He hated no one, at the most crucial point in his life, **I** felt. He had a right to hate them, but He loved them enough to ask God to forgive them and *"Bless them that curse you."* (Luke 6:28) Remember the name of the book is "An Absolute Contradiction". Someone may curse you, but you are operating in the spirit, will utilize the principles and examples of Jesus, may now, turn and bless them. The Bible says, *"Do good to them that hate you and pray for the one who use and persecutes you"* (Matthew 5:44 b)

Why should I? That ye may be the children of your Father which is in Heaven. (Matthew 5:45 a)

Jesus exemplified all teachings when he gave his life to his enemies as a sacrifice of sin. That even unto his death he loved them, knowing they were not worthy.

And we deny, betray, crucify, put him back on the cross daily with the sins we commit. Though he may have felt our actions did not deserve his sacrifice, He felt it worthy to be a propitiation of sin for us. A bridge for us to cross over that would present us faultless before God. That it would be worthy to him that his birth, living, crucifixion, dying and ascension would allow us to be with God, if we only believe.

Christ Jesus knew his enemies. When <u>we</u> know who our enemies are, <u>we</u> want nothing to do with them; nevertheless, Jesus instructs us to love and pray. For God is love. It is impossible to truly love God with our whole heart, when part of our heart has enmity towards those we see daily and have opportunity to forgive, and we don't.

The absolute contradiction is not doing what we feel we should do because it makes us feel good - but to do what God says, though it may hurt our pride. Two things we must remember, 1. God's ways are not like ours and 2. Pride comes before the fall.

The physical body is weak, but those who try hard to operate in the spirit are strong. As a result, we can forgive because we are operating in the spirit and not fulfilling the desires of our weak flesh. We may want to curse someone and not bless them but as said in Proverbs 3:6b *"lean not to thine own understanding"*. We know the enemy has caused us too much pain, but you have to trust God to forgive.

Being able to get to this point means that we have chosen **not** to conform to this world and are at the point of renewing our minds and can present ourselves sacrificially which is our reasonable service and is acceptable to God. Praying for your enemies; It's not **An Absolute Contradiction.**

I Thought it was An Absolute Contradiction

Use these pages to write your version of what you may have thought was an absolute contradiction as it relates to this chapter. Think about after reading this chapter how you would talk with someone about the chapter topic.

Margaret A. Donaldson Cobb

CHAPTER 2: JOY IN THE MIDST OF SORROW

I dedicated this chapter to a special family who lost a young loved one to the violence in the streets. When I went to see the mother after hearing of the tragedy; we were outside talking and crying, across the street a couple was laughing and singing as they were planting flowers. Joy did not know sorrow was having a problem.

The time when you can witness joy and sorrow the most is at a wake and funeral. Though hearts are breaking with sorrow, someone can mention something funny about the deceased that may you start laughing. Or just mention how the deceased touched a life and brought joy to it.

Lost Hope
Ezekiel 19 teaches us about a mother who raised her oldest son to be strong and powerful and once the nations heard of him, they rose against him. Once she heard of the tragedy, **her hope was lost**. The mother had a second son and raised him up in the same manner and the nations again rose against her second son to the point that his voice should no more be heard and again **her hope was lost**.

Ezekiel 19 describes the mother as like a vine in thy blood, planted by the waters, fruitful, and full of branches. She had strong rods for scepters, her stature was exalted among the thick branches. In other words, she was a strong mother. But with all that, because of the tragedies of the sons she had raised, her life was forever changed.

She was plucked in fury, thrown down on the ground, the east wind dried her fruit and the strong rods she had, were broken, they withered and the fire consumed them. After this, the Bible said, she is now planted in the wilderness, a dry and thirsty ground. Probably others who had lost hope were thrown in this dry wilderness and thirsty ground as well.

Found Hope
Ezekiel 37: 1 -5 (paraphrased)- the *hand of the Lord was upon the Son of Man as God placed him in the midst of this valley of dry bones. And as he passed through the valley that was very dry, he passed someone with just enough strength and breath to ask the question "Can these dry bones live?" The answer received was "O, Lord God, thou knowest. Then this weak voice asked the Son of Man to prophesy to these dry bones.* The result of his faith was that life was restored.

Ezekiel 37:11 - once his life was restored, he saw others and realized that "whole house" of Israel was dry. <u>Look, they all are saying</u> "Our bones are dried up and **our hope is lost**; we are cut off for our parts". In my sanctified imagination I can picture this mother who was strong and lost her hope when she lost her boys, in the midst of the valley of dry bones and was raised up with the others and life was restored to her.

As of today, I have not experienced the tragedy of losing a child. But as I read in this story in book of Ezekiel, though the tragedy was great but for this mother the pain was greater. The absolute contradiction people would have you to think is that God will not hear your cry. But I challenge you to cry out to God and he will hear your cry. And God will restore hope and joy.

When the young mother I knew, lost her 15 years old, the funeral was full of young people crying out not understanding the finality and eternity of death. Final on earth, eternal for him who was saved and knew Christ. I too asked God, why? He took me to the book of Ecclesiastes 3:1 *"To everything there is a season and a time to every purpose under Heaven."* I understood that, but what about the ones who may not. God referred me to Isaiah chapter six, where in the year that the King Uzziah died, Isaiah saw the Lord high and lifted up. When God took this young man home, the children and it was hundreds gathered, and those who listened and those who may have never acknowledge God, had to see that He was in charge. As when the king died, our son and friend died, we saw God high and lifted up. The youth choir began to sing, hallelujah, salvation, and glory. The Lord our God, he is wonderful. And there was much sorrow, that song brought out a joyful praise to God, from those who believed.

Unbelievable Sorrow Unbelievable Joy

As I watch the tragedies all over this world, slavery, holocaust, Martin Luther King's death, The Kennedy brothers, the young girls in Alabama, Columbine, The Federal Building bombing in Oklahoma, New York World Trade Center - 9-11 killings and many more. My heart ached for the families and the sadness they felt and probably are still feeling today. I prayed and prayed not understanding and being totally in disbelief that this was happening. For some of these tragedies I either read or heard about them through history. But the New York World Trade Center tragedy on 9-11, I was watching. I was glued to the television, and I saw the second plane hit the second tower. "Oh my God!!!" I hollered. I remember being in front of the television for two weeks straight, paralyzed from the time I got home from work till I went to bed. When my family told me to stop watching the news and the commentaries, I went to the internet. Since I started writing this book so many more unbelievable sorrows have happened; but know that you will find unbelievable joy.

What I realized was that my heart hurt for the family in sadness, but then it would rejoice when I heard a sound of joy. A praise to God for their loved one's life. I would read all about the people and how much joy they brought to others. I know there are a lot of people who are functioning, and some are not - my prayer is that they find strength in the Lord and there they will find "joy in the midst of sorrow".

Unexpected Interruptions
Another time you can witness joy in the midst of what was designed to be sorrowful is when a job comes to an end unexpectedly. I recall working for Sprint Services. They shut the phones off and re-routed our calls to another location just to tell us that our service area will be closing in 7 months and that we had the rest of the day off with pay. Half the folks just about broke down like they said the office was closing that day, the rest of us went to lunch and to the mall. Not to make small of losing a good job, what I have learned in this life is there is a brighter side to everything, if we look for it.

Unexpected Interruption can Cause Sorrow or Renewed Joy
I appreciated this man so much who was affected by the Enron breakdown. Though he lost much money he said, "We will survive, God will take care of us." When you

realize where your true source comes from then you can in so many ways say as Job said in ***Job 13:15***, "though he slay me, yet will I trust him." Joy comes from God. One would think to be joyful is to be happy but to be happy is the result of something happening. The world defines happiness. A new car can only make you happy until the first payment or breakdown. A new house does bring happiness, but a tornado will bring destruction and sorrow. Graduating from school can bring happiness, but what if there is no job to go to after that? If nothing is happening, then what is there to be happy about. Place your eyes on things that are eternal. The Bible says in, "Nehemiah 8:10 ...the joy of the Lord is my strength." John 14:27 speaks on the joy that Jesus gives, the world didn't give it and the world can't take it away.

You may have been encouraged and in turn encouraged someone with this phrase, "God will not put on you more than what you can bear." (1 Corinthians 10:13) Have you ever been down to the point of what you thought was, the end? Daily it seemed to be something attacking you and daily you had to get up with the determination to start all over again. Not realizing that the trials were to strengthen your faith that God would see you through.

When I believe that all things were possible with God and trouble was not to stay but to pass, I felt as though I could go on a little further. I started writing I Thought it was An Absolute Contradiction in 2008. I have had some major losses since that time, losing my mother-in-love in 2011, my husband of thirty-seven years in 2016, my dad in 2020, one of my closest best friends of forty years in 2021 and my sister-in-law who I traveled with three days before she passed. I missed them and I am sad at times, but the joy of knowing them and having great memories keeps me going.

My trials hurt, made me worry, made me sad when I looked at how things were affecting my family, but God, sent joy into our situations and we made it through, joyfully. **And *I thought it was an absolute contradiction.***

I Thought it was An Absolute Contradiction

Use these pages to write your version of what you may have thought was an absolute contradiction as it relates to this chapter. Think about after reading this chapter how you would talk with someone about the chapter topic.

CHAPTER 3: GIVE TO RECEIVE

My last dime! "I know" All I have is my tithe. "That's mine anyway." I have to live for another two weeks. "How did you make it the last two weeks." I just don't have what they have. "Whatcha got?" I can't give like they can. "It's not in equal giving, it's in equal sacrifice." Another offering - ah man. "Walk by faith and not by sight." This was a conversation in church one Sunday between God and me. Who do you think won and who do you think was blessed?

My state of being was "broke" my state of mine was "blessed" the reality was, I did not have any money other than my tithe and offerings, my confession was that "I was never going to be broke another day in my life." The enemy's voice said, "well if you give all you have today you will be broke, today." I almost listened. Then God said, "give and you shall receive." The result of obedience in listening to God was, he blessed me the same day ten-fold of my tithe.

I was in a bookstore and came across some literary work that contradicted God's economic plan of tithing. My first reaction was to respond, my second thought was God will deal with the author. What I have learned is, God's ways are not our ways and not leaning to our own understanding is being understood more and more. I guess the author felt it necessary to write such a book was doing just that, leaning too much on themselves and not God.

Tithing is not just giving God a dime out of every dollar he gives to you. That is the least God asks of us. Tithing is a form of worship. When we worship God, we give to God. Luke 6:38 says, "give and it shall be given unto you". Unfortunately, there is a great debate on tithing; does God say to do so? And who are we tithing to? What are they doing with the money? True enough, people may misappropriate funds, but that is on them and his or her consequences and not for me to judge. I am trusting God on tithing, I know it works, I've tested God a long time ago, and I will continue to give to a giving, loving God. Try it for yourself, read it for yourself. I know, you think or thought that giving is or was an absolute contradiction.

Malachi 3:10 says *"to bring ye all the tithes."*

This statement is for all those who may believe in God and may give money to a t.v. ministry and feel they don't have to come to church to worship God. The word says bring not send. So how can you bring your tithes? Well first you have to bring yourself.

"Into the storehouse." I am not saying don't support other churches, but your tithe should go to the building up of your local church.

The Bible says to store your treasures up in heaven. The closest place to Heaven is not the bank, it's not under your mattress, it's not in the basement under papers in the cedar chest; the closest place is the church.

"That there maybe meat in mine house." This is God speaking, his house is the church and if we bring to the church our tithes and offering, then there is meat in God's house to do

ministry. Feed the hungry. Pay a utility bill. Help children go to college. Buy church vans to go pick up those who can't or don't drive. Pay the bills of the church. Pay those that work in the church that the work of the church would go forth. Vacation Bible School and other programs are not cheap nor free.

"AND PROVE ME NOW HEREWITH SAITH THE LORD OF HOST." Look at God. He trusts in the plan that He created in such a way that He dares you to try it. Prove me, he said. The song says you can't beat God giving no matter how you try. So, try it. Try it more than one time.

"If I will not open you up the windows of heaven and pour you out blessings that there shall not be room enough to receive." You know what this tells me? It tells me that God will bless you with so much that you will have much to share with others. You will be giving out of your excess. I suggest you open the windows.

What I have learned about tithing and giving to God is that it may not always come back monetarily. The result of tithing goes on to say in verse 11, that *"God will rebuke the devourer and he shall not destroy the fruit of your ground..."* During the hardest trials of our lives, the devourer was at work. Taking from the house, bills not being paid the way they should, the cankerworm was trying to take all that it could from us. But I tried my best to be diligent with the tithe and as a result we grew stronger in Christ. There may have been despairing times, but we were not destroyed. And we had peace, hope and joy through it all.

Verse 12 says that *"all the nations will call you blessed, and you shall be a delightsome land."* They may talk about you for giving to your church, but they will also call you blessed. What makes you blessed is that even when things are going in the opposite direction of favor you are still favored. And when folks look at you when things are going one way but you're going God's way; they may view your situation as a negative, and you view it as a positive because you know different.

What do you mean? Glad you asked. I mean that when your house goes into foreclosure, and you had to move. They may talk, did you see she lost her house while she is giving all that money to the church. And you say, but God will give me something better. You may have lost your car but did not lose your mine and can still get to where you need to be. The list can go on. What I realize is people will always view your situation on how it looks, but I would rather it looks like I am losing all I have with God than to think I am gaining or winning with the devil. Because even though it may look like I am losing with God in all actuality I am gaining with God.

What's the name of the book **"I THOUGHT IT WAS AN ABSOLUTE CONTRADICTION"?**

Drop down to verses 16-17. Those who fear God and spoke of Him often to one another (gave praise to God in their circumstance) He hearkened, which means he listened and not only did he listen, but he remembered it. When the praises go up the blessings come down. In verse 17 God has considered you to be one of his and is picking out the jewels for your crown when you get to heaven. He spared your life because you served him in the tithe.

The benefit of tithing is in verse 18: *"Then ye shall return and discern between the righteous and the wicked, between him that serves God and him that serves not God."* We can't beat God giving no matter how we try.

Treat your time and talents as tithes and offering. Giving back to God what he has given you. If God has gifted you to preach, then preach in season and out of season. If God has gifted you to teach, then you are to teach others. Can you sing? Then why are you sitting in the audience? The choir is looking for more gifted singers. What has God gifted you with that you can use to edify the body of Christ?

Now you have your money, time and talents. Really this one should be first and then the others would be no problem and that is to give God your life. Heaven rejoices when one comes into the body of Christ, the citizenship of the kingdom is increased, the neighborhood value rose when you moved in. The benefit in <u>giving</u> your life is that the favor of God will be upon you and don't be misunderstood...the Absolute Contradiction is **Favor ain't fair** to those who knew you when. You will have to explain to them, "favor ain't fair, but it started before I was a seed planted in my mother's womb. And regardless of what sin my life <u>**was**</u> consumed with prior to today, I am confident of this very thing, that he which has began a good work in me will perform it until the day of Jesus Christ."

Giving to receive God's way is not an absolute contradiction.

Margaret A. Donaldson Cobb

I Thought it was An Absolute Contradiction

Use these pages to write your version of what you may have thought was an absolute contradiction as it relates to this chapter. Think about after reading this chapter how you would talk with someone about the chapter topic.

_____

_____

_____

_____

_____

_____

_____

_____

_____

_____

_____

_____

_____

_____

_____

_____

_____

_____

_____

_____

Margaret A. Donaldson Cobb

CHAPTER 4: FROM THE GUTTERMOST TO THE UTTERMOST

I have known people to be down so low that their only home was the gutter. They were in no condition to lift themselves up until one day when Jesus came through, called their name and when he called, they heard, responded and believed in his covenant, never to leave them or forsake them, and now they can stand. Some stand in the pulpit, stand on the doors of the church, in the choir and stand for the one who saved their soul.

Romans 10: 12 -13 *For there is no difference between the Jew and the Greek; for the same Lord over is rich unto all that call upon. For* <u>**WHOSOEVER**</u> *shall call upon the name of the Lord shall be saved.*

Romans 11: 4-15 *But what saith the answer of God unto him? I have reserved to myself seven thousand men, who have not bowed their knee to the image of Baal. Even so then at this present time also there is a remnant according to the election of grace. And if by grace, then is it no more of works; otherwise, grace is no more grace. But if it be of works, then is it no more grace. What then? Israel hath not obtained that which he seeketh for; but the election hath obtained it, and the rest were blinded. (According as it is written, God hath given them the spirit of slumber, eyes that they should not see and ears that they should not hear;) unto this day. And David saith, Let their table be made a snare and a trap and a stumbling block and recompense unto them. Let their eyes be darkened that they may not see and bow down their back alway. I say then,* **Have they stumbled that they should fall?** *God forbid;* <u>but rather through their fall salvation is come unto the Gentiles</u>, *for to provoke them to jealousy. Now if the fall of them* *be the riches of the world, and the diminishing of them the riches of the Gentiles; how much more their fulness? For I speak to you Gentiles, inasmuch as I am an apostle of the Gentiles, I magnify mine office; If by any means I may provoke to emulation them which are my flesh and might save some of them.* **FOR IF THE CASTING DOWN OF THEM BE THE RECONCILING OF THE WORLD, WHAT SHALL THE RECEIVING OF THEM BE, BUT LIFE FROM THE DEAD.**

If you have fallen into the gutter, by choice or not and you find yourself in the lowest state of life and grace seems to not abound, (but you know a little bit about grace); though you are down but have not totally bowed down to the image of Satan so low that you can't see nor hear and at the right time someone comes by and shared Christ with you and they provoked you to want to rise. All because of the grace and the salvation of the Lord. Whereby you were once cast down, you're now given another chance from God who reached down and rescued you back from death, now has given you new life. **An Absolute Contradiction.**

For this chapter I could have re-typed the entire book of Romans. What you will find in this book of the Bible is hope, deliverance, reconciliation, salvation and much more. Tailor-made for one who has a desire to turn their life completely around. It's for those who have slid forward in church, and we missed them sliding back out the doors. This book is written for those who may have never had a relationship with God. Separated at birth never having the chance to meet God because no one cared to introduce them to God. Its purpose is to those who are separated from Him will connect and those who claim that nothing will separate them from Him will be strengthen.

I Thought it was An Absolute Contradiction

Romans 5:8 says, *"while **WE** were yet sinners, Christ died for us."* Those who allow people to keep them down must understand that *Romans 6:23 says, "**ALL** have sin and have fallen short of God's glory."*

The understanding from the book of Romans is that even while you were, or you still maybe "in the gutter" God was and is with you. What seems to be an absolute contradiction here is, those who were **dead** in sin are now **alive** with Christ and not ashamed to proclaim the gospel of Him who save their soul.

It is a mind renewing experience. It is a belief process. It gives power immediately and boldness to proclaim the message of love, hope and deliverance.

Once Romans 12: 1 - 2 has taken place, Romans 10: 9-10 will be a piece of cake. Then expect Acts 1:8 to be your desire to do the will of God in Matthew 28: 18 - 20.

Romans 12: 1-2 I beseech you therefore, brethren, by the mercies of God, that ye present your bodies a living sacrifice, holy and acceptable unto God which is your reasonable service. And be not conformed to this world; but be ye transformed by the renewing of your mind, that ye may prove what is that good and acceptable and perfect will of God.

Romans 10: 9-10 That if thou shall confess with thy mouth and believe in thine heart that God hath raised him from the dead, thou shalt be saved. For with the heart man believeth unto righteousness; and with the mouth confession is made unto salvation.

Acts 1:8 But ye shall receive power after that the Holy Ghost is come upon you and ye shall be witnesses unto me both in Jerusalem and in all Judea and in Samaria and unto the uttermost part of the earth.

Matthew 28:18 -20 And Jesus came and spoke saying, All power is given unto me in Heaven and in earth. Go ye therefore and teach all nations, baptizing them in name of the Father and of the Son and of the Holy Ghost; Teaching them to observe all things whatsoever I have commanded you; and lo, I am with you alway, even unto the end of the world.

You will find yourself testifying about what God has done for you. Where you were once a sinner, now you're a sinner SAVED by grace, equipped, and wearing the armor of God to go out and evangelize. The contradiction here is, that you may make the "church folk" uncomfortable.

Evangelize!!! Yes evangelize. Evangelism can be simply defined as, communicating the good news, the gospel of Jesus Christ. After all, he did save your soul. So, tell it.

The writer of Romans and the writer of the majority of the New Testament name is Paul. He was known before his life change as Saul. What you must realize is that Saul hated Jesus. He killed for people just calling on the name of Jesus. But God set out to find Saul and when he did his mind was changed to love God and God changed his name to Paul. Saul, who is now Paul is an apostle. Teaching about Jesus. Read Acts 9: 1 - 28; it may seem to be contradictory to us, because when God converts people we know like that, we may not want to believe it, see it and especially hear it.

For the modern-day Paul's and Paula's, persecution comes when you decide to do the right thing. When the good that's in you wants to come out and you let it, folks will surely begin persecuting you. But the hope of God is, that all would be saved. I know you can't believe that all the hell you have raised, things you have done, said, heard and repeated, all that you have stolen from others and maybe have slain, and I don't mean in the spirit. All the drugs and alcohol you were big enough to consume that did not kill you. All the people you have been with and you're free from infection. You have taken matters into your own hands and other things that you have done, you can only tell God; and with your confession and belief, all that is thrown in God's sea of forgetfulness. You lived long enough to give your sins to the one who knew no sin but died for sin that you might live.

Maybe you were born in a house that was covered by the blood of Jesus. Because Grandma, Papa, Big Momma's, Auntie, Uncle's somebody's prayer God showed favor to you by not allowing the plagues of depression, drugs, alcohol, promiscuity, shame, illnesses, all manner of sin to overtake your life to death. God allowed you to overcome that you might witness about the goodness of the Lord. Humbling yourselves and praying, seeking God's face and turning from your wicked ways; then God will hear from heaven, forgiving you of your sin and will heal your land. That's favor. And to those who don't want to believe how God can take a mess and bless it to his glory; then to others, favor is an absolute contradiction and it ain't fair.

Margaret A. Donaldson Cobb

I Thought it was An Absolute Contradiction

Use these pages to write your version of what you may have thought was an absolute contradiction as it relates to this chapter. Think about after reading this chapter how you would talk with someone about the chapter topic.

Margaret A. Donaldson Cobb

CHAPTER 5: FINE DECEPTION

This chapter's Bible reference comes from the Book of Ezekiel Chapter 17. In this lesson you will find deception in the example of two eagles. An eagle that was strong, confident, wealthy and was oh so fine. The other eagle was watching him and the lust of the eye clouded her vision. What you will learn as you read the scriptures and my revelation is that the eagle could be a classic case of someone you may know who has deceived you and your family with their looks, things, smooth talk, money and their power or so-called-power. This is how drug dealers move in, master manipulators cause your children to be deceive and make decisions about life that is detrimental to them. It's how we fall in the snares of the evil one. In this story the fine-deceptive eagle has a male dominant characteristic and the second eagle a female. But don't be deceived it can easily be reversed.

Ezekiel 17.**SPEAKING TO THE HOUSE**: *And sometimes that "ain't" easy*

1 - 2 And the word of the Lord came unto **ME SAYING**; *Son of man, put forth a riddle and* **speak** *a parable unto the house of Israel*

> By the authority vested in me I come to speak a word to the house.
> (Don't get caught up on the gender language- God speaks to whomever is listening)
>
> Speak a parable - give an example to the house - inform them what "thus saith the Lord God"

Verses 3 - 5 The Parable

A great eagle with great wings, long winged, full of feathers, which had divers colours came unto Lebanon and <u>took</u> the highest branch. He cropped off the top of his twigs and carried it into a land of traffic; he set it in a city of merchants. He <u>took</u> also of the seed of the land and planted it in a fruitful field; he placed it by great waters and set it as a willow tree.

> He looked to be powerful, big, decked out in all of his glory and then sat high up so he can be seen. The scripture said "he <u>took</u> the highest branch"

> Then he brought his money - seed - and put where everyone else was selling their own goods could see his. Intimidation.... The scripture said "he set it in" - He didn't buy a thing

> He didn't buy a thing because the scripture said after that "he <u>took</u> also of the seed of the land and placed in his field - where he knew it would grow and bring forth fruit.

Verse 6

And it grew; and became a spreading vine of <u>low stature</u>, whose branches turned toward him, and the roots thereof were under him; so, it became a vine - and brought forth branches and shot forth sprigs.

> It did grow - became a wide vine

> But it was of low stature - it spread - it did not grow upward

The branches turned toward him - instead of God - they grew but under him

It became a vine - a vine with branches and sprigs - it didn't say a vine with fruit. Which he just **"knew it would grow and bring forth fruit"** Verse 6

Verse 7 - 8 Another Parable

There was also another great eagle with wings and many feathers; and behold this vine did bend her roots toward him and shot forth branches toward him that he might water it by the furrows of her plantation. It was planted in a good soil by great waters that it <u>might</u> bring forth branches and that it <u>MIGHT</u> bear fruit; that it <u>might</u> be a <u>goodly vine</u>.

The female eagle - was watching and was influenced by what she saw
Without question wanted him to plant her roots and water it, not knowing that his did not grow or produce fruit. And he planted it in what was supposed to be good ground.

Be careful of what you see someone else do. Be mindful of the seeds you plant; even though you may plant a seed in good ground - depending on the type of seed; it still may not grow.

Verses 9 - 10

Say thou, Thus saith the Lord God; Shall it prosper? Shall he not pull up the roots thereof and cut off the fruit there of, that it whither? It shall whither in all the leaves of her spring, even without great powers or any people to pluck it up by the roots thereof.

- Hey, Mr. Fine Deceiver, this is God; that which you have planted will it bear fruit?
- Will you find anything roots, fruit or will it have withered before it had a chance to grow?
- While everything else in the field is growing, this will die before the mighty one or people get a chance to pluck it up. Just because it was planted, does that mean it will prosper?

Understanding God can be confusing. Sometimes when you read and try to understand what he is saying, it could be quite contrary to what you see or even hear and try to understand for yourself. *In this parable the absolute contradiction is that a seed was planted in good ground. Ground where it was sure to grow, and it didn't.* Read deeper. It's not that the seed would not grow; it is how the seed was planted and the way in which it grew. You can't grow something that is not yours. The description given about the sower of this seed was that it was - strong, mighty, wealthy and was a <u>taker</u>. "It took" the scripture said. Could go wherever it wanted to go and show itself off to be great. So convincing that without thought, others gave their seed to it, not knowing who they were giving their seed to.

So many times, we get tricked because of what we have seen. So many times, one who is stronger, more powerful / influential, great in wealth can impress us on one hand and intimidate is on the other, then we find ourselves trapped. But when we know the strong, more powerful and wealthy for who they really are and how they really achieved their wealth, then we understand that, it's just what it looks like and not what it really is. The bad part about this is that so many followers of Christ fall in this trap. Then we feel taken advantage of. Someone took from us and promised us and would not keep their promise and now we have nothing and are destitute to the point that we can't move. The Bible says, "let no man deceive you."

Ezekiel 17 STILL SPEAKING TO THE HOUSE

Verse 11 - 13

Moreover, the word of the Lord came unto ME saying: Say now to the rebellious house, Know ye not what these things mean? Tell them; Behold, the king of Babylon is to come to Jerusalem and hath taken the king thereof and the princes thereof and led them with him to Babylon; And hath taken the king's seed and made a covenant with them and taken an oath of him: he hath also taken the mighty of the land: That the kingdom <u>might be base</u>, that it might not lift itself up, but by keeping of his covenant it might stand.

>The strong, mighty and wealthy are on their way.
>They're coming to take away the head of the family.
>They want your children.
>They want to take them to their territory.
>They are coming for your seed's seed promising them wealth quickly - false wealth. Smiling at them with gold, silver, or platinum teeth instead of white teeth. Showing them what <u>their</u> wealth looks like trying to convince them that they are for real.
>
>They also want all those who are in covenant with God. The very elect of God. That they are maybe so weak and cannot lift themselves up.

The absolute contradiction comes after the "but by keeping" in verse 13 but by keeping God's covenant and believing that He will never leave us no forsake us; with that, we might stand.

It's a known fact that the enemy comes to rob, steal, kill and destroy. If the enemy can achieve this goal by taking everyone that is strong, mighty and wealthy in the things of God and convinced them with a promise that his way is better, then the rest of the family becomes weak.

It's like the modern-day family. If the head of the family is weak, missing in action and believing lies of the destroyer; it might be able to destroy you, your seed and your seed's seed. Keep God's covenant and stand against the wiles of the "Fine Deceiver."

I THOUGHT IT WAS AN ABSOLUTE CONTRADICTION

I Thought it was An Absolute Contradiction

Use these pages to write your version of what you may have thought was an absolute contradiction as it relates to this chapter. Think about after reading this chapter how you would talk with someone about the chapter topic.

Margaret A. Donaldson Cobb

CHAPTER 6: THE FOOLISHNESS OF PREACHING

*F**aith comes by hearing but how can I get faith unless I hear someone preach or teach it. There have been days that hope was gone, I stepped in church and testimony service was going on. Sistergirl's testimony was my testimony and because she had heard a crazy preacher preach she had hope and because I heard her testimony I received hope. Then I passed that same hope on to someone else; faith really can come by just hearing*

1 Corinthians 1:17 - 21 *For Christ sent me not to baptize but to preach the gospel: not with wisdom of words, lest the cross of Christ should made of none effect. For the preaching of the cross is to them that perish* **foolishness**: *but unto us which are saved it is the power of God. For it is written, I will destroy the wisdom of the wise and will bring to nothing the understanding of the prudent. Where is the wise? Where is the scribe? Where is the disputer? Hath not God made foolish the wisdom of the world? For after that in the wisdom of God, the world by wisdom knew not God,* **it pleased God by the foolishness of preaching** *to save them that believe.*

Romans 1:20 - 22 *For the invisible things of him from the creation of the world are clearly seen, being understood by the things that are made, even his eternal power and Godhead; so that they are without excuse. Because that, when they knew God, they glorified him not as God, neither were thankful; but became vain in their imaginations and their foolish heart was darkened. Professing themselves to be wise they became fools.*

An absolute contradiction: The wise can be seen as foolish and the foolish can be seen as wise.

Don't impress people with your wisdom - because they will just remember your wisdom and knowledge of words - but the foolishness of preaching is where you decrease your flesh and allow God to speak through you that he might be glorified will result in one's life being save because you preached not yourself but Him and Him alone.

I more than anyone desires for the preacher to be educated. I don't want someone leading me who cannot rightly divide the Word of truth. But more than that I want you to have all your credentials to lead the people first with your B.A. Degree and that is to be Born Again. Coupling your wisdom with a testimony, that without God, you are nothing.

As a called fellow-worker of the gospel with more education than some not as much as many, but chosen nonetheless, will not contradict the word of God by thinking that I am all that, lest I fall on my face.

We who are called, chosen, claim to know God, have been hearing about God should know that God is not rude. We are instructed to be careful how we speak to people. I witnessed a lady talking down to a teenager (after church) about the outfit she had on. I personally felt like saying something to contradict the woman, even though she was correct in her thoughts, it was how she said it that made me mad and uncomfortable for the young lady. But that would have been an example of vengeance, so the Lord shut my mouth and told me to pray.

There are so many people who are unchurched now because of something someone said. "The power of life and death is in the tongue" and though it happens daily, the word says the bitter and sweet can't come out of the same fountain. James 3:14

Isaiah 50: 4 - 10 gives wisdom to those of us who have been in church for years. *"The Lord God hath given me the tongue of the <u>learned</u>, that I should know how to speak a word in season to him that is weary; he wakeneth morning by morning, he wakeneth mine ear to hear as the learned."*

The weary have to press on to the next day like we do. If last night was not their last night and though tomorrow is not promised, but it's on its way; if we have "the learned" have spoken to them with wisdom, clarity and an encouraging word; then just maybe they can make it through another day.

Colossians 4: 2 - 6 *Continue in prayer and watch in the same with thanksgiving; Withal praying also for us, that God would open unto us a door of utterance, to speak the mystery of Christ, for which I am also in bonds. That I may make it manifest, as I ought to speak; Walk in wisdom toward them that are without, redeeming the time; Let your speech be always with grace, seasoned with salt, that ye may know how you ought to answer every man.*

If the weary are now encouraged, then continue to pray for them. Pray for yourself that arrogance and judgement won't get in your way and when God opens a door for us to speak, make sure you speak praise only unto Him. Walk with them who seemed to be less fortunate, hurting, unlearned, the left behind, the left out, the left alone or the lied on. The least, the last, the lost, the un-liked, the locked up and locked out may have hope. When they question you about life, speak with boldness, but ever so kind that they will taste and see how good God really is. And because you have spoke with kindness and they have heard you, then their faith is increased. Remember Romans 8:17 says, *"faith comes by hearing, and by hearing the word of God."*

Isaiah 61:1 - 2a *The Spirit of Lord God is upon me; because the Lord hath anointed me preach the good tidings unto the meek; he hath sent me to bind the broken hearted, to proclaim liberty to the captive and the opening of prison to them that are bound. To proclaim the acceptable year of the Lord and the day of vengeance of our God......*

Your reaction to that scripture maybe, "God called me!!!" Before you get too excited remember that many are called, only a few are chosen. True enough you can be called. I believed that all who hear the word of God and who have believed the word of God and has been in church for years are called to ministry. But the ones who have the work of ministry in their hearts have availed themselves to go higher in Christ, are the chosen.

The absolute contradiction maybe that God would not use the one with all the credentials, degrees in counseling, ordained, to preach to the drug addict, by one God has delivered and called them to preach. It's not that God did not see the one, but he chose the one he wanted, because wisdom was not the need at the time - a witness DELIVERED from drugs was the need. Romans 10:8 says *"But what saith it? The word is nigh thee, even in thy mouth and in thy heart; that is, the word of faith which we preach."* So, if deliverance is to come, it matters not that a degree has not yet been obtained but that the word would be in your mouth and in your heart. And has been confessed in a way that righteousness and salvation is upon you.

The Result of the foolishness of Preaching Jesus

Isaiah 61: 2b - 5 ...to comfort all that mourn. To appoint unto them that mourn Zion. to give unto them beauty of ashes, the oil of joy for mourning, the garment of praise for the spirit of heaviness; that they might be called trees of righteous, the planting of the Lord that he might be glorified.

And they shall build the old wastes, they shall raise up the former desolations and they shall repair the waste cities, the desolations of many generations.

And strangers shall stand and feed your flocks, and the sons of alien shall be your plowmen and vinedressers.

The Absolute Contradiction to the world:

> The meek will gain strength.
> Broken hearts will be mended.
> Freedom will come to those who are bound physically.
> To the bound that they may be freed mentally because they heard about God and now, they are in perfect peace.
> In sorrow, those that mourn will be comforted.
> The ones who dirtied the streets are now the ones who cleans the streets.
> The stranger you fed will come and feed you.
> Some employers will be inspired to hire one that was then considered unrighteous but is now considered righteous.

> The mystery of Christ that was once a secret is now revealed.

> Confession of Christ that he was crucified, died, and rose that righteousness and salvation is for all who have sinned and fallen short of God's glory.

If ever I get the chance to preach / teach this chapter. I would start off with this thought.

The absolute contradiction relating to the "foolishness of preaching" is people would be doing exactly what we say, instead of doing what they see us do. We are so apt to do what we see others do; instead of listening to what they have said.

> Example: If a young child who watches everything sees you smoking. You tell him or her that they should not smoke because it's bad for your health. They may ask, "well why are you smoking if its bad for their health?" And your response maybe, "just do what I said, and not as I do."

At this point and time in life you can make the difference in your child's life, whether he or she becomes a smoker or not. If they see you practicing what you preach, then they might believe what you have said.

> Another example: Let's say, your marriage comes to an end right when your daughter is about to be old enough to date. You have strict rules in this area hoping to protect her from being hurt or promiscuous. Now until this point in life she listens to you but, you've started dating again. And

everything you told her not to do, you do it in her presence. What do you think she will think as she is watching you?

The cliche' "the fruit don't fall far from the tree" well you can best believe in this day and time you will hear, "well Mommy, I'm just doing what you are doing." And your walk coupled with your talk could save her life. Remember she is watching you and seeing you respect yourself, set strict rules for yourself, then your child might believe that you believe in your own words.

In the beginning God did not do anything, he said it. He said, "let there be light" and there was light. (Genesis 1:3) "The power of life and death is in the tongue". (Proverbs 18:21) Moses did what God said, and as a result the Israelites were set free. Though they murmured in the wilderness, especially when Pharoah's army was on their trail, the red sea in front of them; Moses kept what God said in his heart. Though his faith may have wavered - he heard what the God of Abraham, Issac and Jacob told him what to do. As a result, folks walked on ground that should have been too muddy to walk on, but it was dry.

I like Joshua. Moses is dead now and he was to be the leader of the people. And just like today when the new people are placed in charged, they have to make a speech. Told the people to go on over the Jordan. He said, that wherever they placed the sole of their feet they were going to prosper. Now pay close attention: IT'S WHAT HE SAID! Joshua preached about the one he believed in and told the people to choose who they were going to serve. Because Joshua said, "for his house they were going to serve the

Lord. Joshua put into action what he was preaching."
(Joshua 24:15)

John the Baptist preached repentance and the remission of sin. The Bible described as one crying in the wilderness preparing a way for the Lord, making his paths straight.
The foolishness of preaching God's words, if properly preached will do at least three things:

>It will make you mindful of your actions.

>It will make you be careful of what you say and how you say it.

>It will make you make a decision.

Action speaks louder than words. Practice what you preach and be careful to make the right choice. If you have to, sacrifice your fleshly pleasures, then do so. The result maybe, the ones who are watching you will do you said, (though to them you may sound foolish), and not what you have done.

I Thought it was An Absolute Contradiction

Use these pages to write your version of what you may have thought was an absolute contradiction as it relates to this chapter. Think about after reading this chapter how you would talk with someone about the chapter topic.

Margaret A. Donaldson Cobb

CHAPTER 7: NO WAY OUT BUT BY ME

I turned to the left and was met with bills not being able to be paid. I turned to the right and the doctor is trying to tell me something I don't want to hear. I try going out the back door and the nay sayers were there taunting me, telling me what I can't do. I see the front door, it looks like it's open, so I run to it and more bad news met me there. AN ABSOLUTE CONTRADICTION. There was no way out until I started to quote: Jesus is the way, no other name under heaven whereby I can be saved. Call on the name of Jesus and ye shall be saved!!! He heard my cry and delivered me from all of my trials.

I want out!

Have you ever felt like you were in a situation that you wanted to get of but, for whatever reason you stayed or are staying? You make up excuses you really don't believe. You may feel sometimes things are too hard and you may never get out. You may have made some mistakes have you trapped and for ego and pride you stay in. When you looked back, you realized the first thing you should have done was to get out. You may want to move, and you don't because you think about others and how they would feel instead of listening to the soft voice inside you.

Excuses for staying in certain situations too long will cause us too much heart ache and unnecessary pain. The peace we often forfeit, the pain we bear needlessly is because we do not carry everything to God in prayer. Unfortunately for us, we stay in situations too long before we realize we need to be out and pay too much with our lives.

We want out of debt. We want out of a relationship that has gone bad. We out of a dead-end job. We want out to get out of trouble. We want to get out of school. We just want out. There are some things in life we can change and get out of but, first it takes a renewing of the mind and having a vision. Hindsight is 20/20; if we had of just thought first by seeking God, we truly would not be in some of the situations we're in or have gone through. But we have to come to the conclusion that it's time to get out. The first step is in the changing of your mind. The enemy would have you think, "This is where God wants me to be." **<u>NO!</u>** 3 John 1:2 says, "Beloved I wish above all things that thou mayest prosper, being health, even as thy soul prospers."

The enemy wants us to feel "we can't". **WRONG!** Phillipians 4:13 says, "I can do all things through Christ which strengthens me."

The reality very well maybe that you are feeling anxious to the point of panic. But God says, Phillipians 4:19 "Be anxious for nothing, but everything with prayer and supplication."

The thought, that we all deal with is thinking, God is not moving fast enough; when we know God's timing is not our timing.

The reality is that we may feel like we're all alone. But when Moses went to Pharoah, he said, "Let my **PEOPLE** go." Not just my man, woman, boy or girl. He said, "my **people**" which is a group.

The title to this chapter, ***"No Way Out but By Me"*** is not so much an absolute contradiction, because Jesus is the only way out. It becomes an absolute contradiction, when your spirit and flesh are at war and the flesh seems to be winning. Galatians 5:17 says, "that the spirit and the flesh are contrary to one another."

Your flesh contributes to the contradiction by the pain it physically feels, your physical sight and the negativity your ears hear.

When I see people crying about the bondage that they are in, I see a cleansing taking place and a renewing of the mind. People may get tired of crying in the wilderness, crying in bondage, crying through the struggle, crying through the pain. But I say, cry; Psalms 126: 5 Says, "They that sow in tears, shall reap in joy,"

When you get sick and tired of being sick and tired; you'll create a path to escape. Throwing out old clothes, old papers, boxing stuff up. You start getting rid of a lot of baggage, things you don't need because they will weigh you down. You'll find your conversation being, though he slay me yet will I trust him. (Job 13:15) You let them take your car, house and you'll say as the scriptures say, "I came in this world naked, and naked shall I go; The Lord gives, and the Lord takes away, blessed be the name of the Lord." (The Book of Job paraphrased). People will begin to say you're crazy, they'll say, "surely thou art mad; you are losing everything." And you tell them to start counting blessings, not with numbers, but with joy. You may have to school them, that in this world you are going to have some trial and tribulations, but you have to be of good cheer. Christ overcame this world and so can we. Next thing you know, you're moving forward. Like the children of Israel followed Moses across the Red Sea and the ground that should have been soggy but God, in Exodus chapter 14, hardened the ground enough for them to walk on.

He's the same God yesterday, today, and forevermore.

Here's another contradiction; when you get out, God may tell you to go back.

How do you think marriages are reconciled? You find yourself going back to a job you left saying, "I'm not doing that again and find yourself doing that same thing over again. The sad part is having the mind of the Israelites. Being ungrateful. God forbid, that they had forgotten, that God delivered them out of bondage. Or maybe the lesson that you were to learn, once you got out, you forgot and now you are back in captivity. Sometimes it's not always the going through praying to get out, it's the lesson learned while you're in it. So, you did not learn your lesson and God placed you back through it again. It's like going through school. For an entire year, you have been learning, but now it's time to take the test; you fail and guess what, you have to repeat that grade.

Lest we forget that it was God that made us, God that saves us, God that delivers us from our own self destruction and we not give him glory, honor and praise; we may find ourselves right back where we started from.

I Thought it was An Absolute Contradiction

Some people once they are delivered have a strong determination not to go back.
Some feel they are strong enough to go back and witness to old friends, maybe family on what the Lord has done and successfully bring others out. But then there are those want to go back but are too weak to stand against the wiles of the devil and find themselves right back in their old circumstance.

The only way out of trouble is to call on the name of the Lord. Jeremiah 33:3 Call on the name of the Lord and ye shall be saved.

Your life was worth saving, for if not, Christ would not have sacrificed his for yours. Even though he knew you he still did what he did for you.

Life is tricky. For if we break the word *"life"* down and take it apart, we see some things in that life without Christ is all about.

LIFE can be an absolute contradiction.

Take away the **"L and E"** you get the word *"if"* I believe that "if" is a choice word, for if I had not made some choices, then I would not be needing Jesus to get me out.

Take out the **"F"** we have the word *"lie"* and lies can put you in a place that they only way out is Jesus.
Scramble the all four letters - you get **"FILE"** Which is what we need. A faith file to show the devil that God has kept you before and he will keep you again.

You may find yourself in too deep and feel that there is no way out. But 2 Chronicles 7:14 says, "if my people who are called by my name would humble themselves and pray, seek my face, turn from their wicked ways, then I will hear from Heaven and heal their land."

Deuteronomy 28 says to .... choose life".
More than anything: Jesus said, "I am the way, the truth and the *life* - no one can get to the Father BUT BY ME".

I Thought it was An Absolute Contradiction

Use these pages to write your version of what you may have thought was an absolute contradiction as it relates to this chapter. Think about after reading this chapter how you would talk with someone about the chapter topic.

Margaret A. Donaldson Cobb

CHAPTER 8: LOVE BEARS ALL

*G**ood times or bad times love can go through. Triumphs and trials love can deal with it. Your child maybe graduating from school or going to jail love handles it. Pleasures of life or disappointments love is in the midst of it all. Pre-med, no mom pre-gnancy, love took a lick but it stills ticks. Baby, I messed up, got another woman but I love you, yeah <u>like</u> may not be around but love is always there.... AN ABSOLUTE CONTRADICTION?*

For thou art an holy people unto the Lord thy God; the Lord thy God hath chosen them to be a special people unto himself, above all people that are upon the face of the earth. "The Lord did not set his love upon you, nor choose you, because ye were more in number than any people; <u>for ye were the fewest of all people.</u> <u>But because the Lord loved you</u>, and because he would keep the oath which he had sworn unto your fathers had the Lord brought you out with a mighty hand and redeemed you out of the house of bondmen, from the hand of Pharaoh King of Egypt." Deuteronomy 7: 6 - 8.

Paul, who was once Saul, killed anyone who proclaimed Christianity, was redeemed because of the love of God as he traveled on the road to Damascas; where he would continue his plight to kill Christians, met God. And because of the love of God his life changed. Where now he is a minister according to the gift of grace from God; proclaimed in Ephesians 3:8 **Unto me, who am <u>less than</u> the least of all saints, is this grace give that I should preach among the Gentiles the unsearchable riches of Christ.**

Our sin separates us from God. God's unconditional love redeems us, because He is love and love bears all things.

The title of this chapter "Love Bears All" fits in the category of being 'An Absolute Contradiction' by that it is a contradiction. For Christ knew his own would hurt his heart and because of his heart for them he died anyway.

As people, we would hurt ones we love and love the ones we hate. Jesus said, you cannot serve two masters, you'll loved one and hate the other.

Love bears all. 1 Corinthians 13:7 It can bear the disappointment of the good, the mistreatment from the bad and the negative attitude from the ugly.

Love can forgive the unforgivable, love the unlovable and reach the unreachable.

Love can just look at you and you straighten up. Love can whip your behind because it was out of order and then sooth it and make it feel better. Love chastises those it loves. Love will go without something for itself, just so you can have. Love will give up it's last dime and all of it's time just so you can achieve your goals.

Have you ever seen love operate? Love had to watch its children get hurt and there was nothing it could do about it. Love watched its children go to jail, ended up in a situation that was unto death and there was nothing it could do about it. Love had to watch a child quit school because they failed or came home pregnant. Love watched the one it loved, walked out on it never to return. Love watched you love someone else who really did not love you and wanted to make it jealous. Love had to bear all of this. Love watched its parents go from in control to, out of control. Love let you mistreat it, talk to it crazy and when it should have knocked you down, it just loved you.

Love. How strong is love? Love is so strong that when *hate* arose against it, hate fell/failed. Love stood strong on that fact that no weapon formed against it was going to prosper. Love realized that in this world it was going to have trial and tribulation and was of good cheer, because it knew it could bear all and over come.

Love works very hard to make sure you have the very best it can give. It's a thankless job, but love can handle it. What's the absolute contradiction about love? Contradiction is the only way it can manifest itself to be seen, touch, and cared for; is to be wrapped in flesh. And we know the flesh is the opposite of love. Flesh hurts, hates and gets angry. Flesh will kill you if you mistreat it. Flesh will leave you if you embarrass it. Flesh hates to see love operate for flesh is a jealous thing. Flesh is not strong, it's weak. The flesh is miserable when love is prospering. The flesh can't handle all things. The flesh retaliates when it's challenged. Even if you were born of the flesh, it will turn on you in a heartbeat. And when you're hurting, flesh laughs at you.

When love came down to earth wrapped up in flesh and started operating in love, flesh could not take it. Flesh beat it unto the death. But since love could bear all things, it allowed the flesh to do just what it wanted to do. Love knew that it would be hated. Love knew it would be lied on, misused, abused to the point of death.

But Love describes itself best in 1 Corinthians 13: 1 – 7.

I can speak to all but if I have not love for them, then I become as brass or tinkling cymbals making a lot of noise. As we use to say, "talking loud and saying nothing."

I am gifted in things of this world and above, I understand things that others can't comprehend, well versed on many things, but without love, I am nothing.

I can feed the poor, give and it does not take away from what I have, but if I do it without love then it profits me nothing.

Though I suffer, I still have to be kind.
Though others can do as I do, I am not to be envious of them.

Though I can, I don't brag or lift myself up.

I behave myself, I look out for others, I'm not easily provoked, nor do I think of evil things.

I don't rejoice when bad things happen to you. I rejoice in truth, that God will help you and provide you a way of escape.

I bear all things. I believe all things really do work together for good, I hope the best for you and I can endure anything you place upon me.

Think on these things when the flesh wars with love. Love is steadfast, unmovable, it always abounds in the work of the Lord. Love is the greatest thing of all. It was love that God sent his son on earth and it was love that his son came.

Who shall separate us from the love of Christ? Shall tribulation, or distress, or persecution or famine, or nakedness, or peril or sword. As it is written, for thy sake, we are killed all day long; we are counted as sheep for the slaughter. Nay, in all these things we are more than conquerors through him that loved us. For I am persuaded that neither death, nor life, nor angels, nor principalities, nor power, nor things present, nor things to come. Nor height, nor depth, nor any other creature, shall be able to separate us from the love of God, which is in Christ Jesus our Lord.

And we know that all things work together for good to them that love God to them who are the called according to his purpose. Especially when all is failing or when feeling extremely sad.

A Love Letter to Sadness – God Inspired

Love knocked on my door one night. I was not expecting any company that night, so I did not open the door. The next morning, I opened the door and found a letter on it. It read, "I saw you were lonely and sad, having dinner by yourself. I thought if I'd knock, you would answer and let me in. I realize every time, here lately, you have opened your door and let someone in, you got hurt.

I know you have had people tell you they loved you and just took advantage of you. I know that some have forced their way in. I have seen your friends come by needing a place to stay and you let them in, and they mistreated you and your house. I know it has been hard watching your children fall by the wayside and you hate you to see them coming to your door; for the only reason they come is because they are in need or in trouble.

I understand, you've had too much to bear. It saddens my heart to see a place once so full of fun, laughter and love, is so lonely now. As a matter of fact, I was feeling a little down myself. Some of the people I have loved the most and I knew they loved me have turned their backs on me. They are mad at me because they wanted some things from me; I felt at the time it was not good for them. And because of that, they are mad. I saw a lady who used to always pray to me for a husband. I was in the process of creating him for her, per her request. I had not heard from her in a very long time, I guess I was taking too long. On my way here to see you, I saw that lady; she had married someone I didn't know and he was abusing her.

I could really tell you a lot more but, my concern is for you. I know you feel you are in the middle of an absolute contradiction, seeing the kind of person you are. I just stopped by to encourage and make you smile again. Take my advice; don't get weary in doing well. The tears you have sown - you'll reap in joy very soon. Think it not strange - stranger things have happened. Hold on your change is coming.

I declared to your forefathers that I would be there for you and I will. Don't be anxious, keep praying. Keep thy heart with all diligence, for out of it flows the issues of life. Be careful, the glory is right around the corner, any little thing might cause you to miss it.

I love you Sadness. I would rather call you Gladness. I hope this letter encourages you and makes you feel better. Oh - I think I see a smile!

Love Ya

J.C. Love -
P.S. Dad says "Hi".

I Thought it was An Absolute Contradiction

Use these pages to write your version of what you may have thought was an absolute contradiction as it relates to this chapter. Think about after reading this chapter how you would talk with someone about the chapter topic.

Margaret A. Donaldson Cobb

CHAPTER 9: THE LEAST OF THEM HAD THE MOST

Melchisdec (Genesis 14:17-20), without father, without mother was blessed. The widow gave more than others because she gave her all.

In the Book of Hebrews 7
¹ For this Melchisedec, king of Salem, priest of the most high God, who met Abraham returning from the slaughter of the kings, and blessed him;
² To whom also Abraham gave a tenth part of all; first being by interpretation King of righteousness, and after that also King of Salem, which is, King of peace.
³ Without father, without mother, without descent, having neither beginning of days, nor end of life; but made like unto the Son of God; abideth a priest continually.
⁴ Now consider how great this man was, unto whom even the patriarch Abraham gave the tenth of the spoils.
⁵ And verily they that are of the sons of Levi, who receive the office of the priesthood, have a commandment to take tithes of the people according to the law, that is, of their brethren, though they come out of the loins of Abraham:
⁶ But he whose descent is not counted from them received tithes of Abraham, and blessed him that had the promises.

⁷And without all contradiction the less is blessed of the better.

Mark 12: 42 – 44 *And there came a certain poor widow, and she threw in two mites, which make a farthing. And he (Jesus) called unto his disciples and saith unto them; verily I say unto you that* **this poor widow hath cast more** *in than all they who have cast into the treasury; For all they did cast in of their abundance, but she of her want did cast in all that she had even all her living.*

You thought you were the least of all so you settled for less. You thought because what you had looked too little in your hands, you did not place in God's hand.

I have not ever made a lot of what people would call "real good money" but I have made enough to take care of three children through some very rough times. I prayed and trusted God through it all and in turn, he took care of us. Regardless of if we had money or not we never missed anything at church. We may not have had much on our pantry, but if I did not have a dollar for them for offering, I told them to get a can good for our church pantry, somebody had less than us. The absolute contradiction for some, especially the well to do, is that God would bless someone like me. Though my things did not cost as much as someone else, I still had what they had. Some people close to me felt I should not have, but they misunderstood God.

When I look back in time, going through the trials with three children, had I not trusted God and kept them close to God, I could have lost them. I am not boasting to brag, I am boasting in God's faithfulness and being a promise keeper.

When you're in a position of "lack" or being or having the least of everyone, know that with God you are multiplied a thousand times. *Deuteronomy 1:11 The Lord God of your fathers makes you a thousand times so many more as ye are and bless you as he hath promised you.* Never underestimate the power of your giving. For giving to God is equal sacrifice. It's in the sacrificial giving where God is trusted and taken seriously. This opens the window of heaven and releases the blessings on your life. All this takes faith and working. For faith, without works is dead and, is impossible to please God. For when you go to him, you must believe that he is and he is a rewarder to them that diligently seek him. (James 2:17) *Now* faith is the substance of things hoped for the evidence of things you cannot see. (Hebrews 11:1) It did not say "then faith" or the "future's faith" it says now.

Overcome lack with faith, giving and receiving. Stay encouraged, regardless of how long it takes; Deuteronomy 2:7 says, *"For the Lord thy God hath blessed thee in all the works of thy hand; he knoweth thy walking through the great wilderness; these forty years the Lord thy God hath been with thee; thou hast lack nothing."*

The name of the book is called, "An Absolute Contradiction" but with God (the equalizer), all can be gathered together. The "lackers" and slackers. The rich and the poor. The good and the bad. The "haves" and the "have nots." The educated and the not-so-educated. For in the eyes of God, there are no differences.

Overcoming Lack - *Reaping and sowing - sowing and reaping. The more you plant the greater your harvest.*
Contrary to popular belief, what you see is what you get. But to the believer of Christ, what you don't see is what you

get. Once you plant something you can't see it until it starts to grow. If you never nurture it, add something to it, feed it, water it, claim it by talking to it - it may never grow. It's like a garden, children, marriage, money, your job/business or anything you want to grow. If it's lacking anything, take a good look at what it is you are not doing. It's a true act of faith. A true sower walks by faith and not by sight. There are so many types of seeds we can plant. Turn your lack into a seed of what you need.

My God will supply all of your needs according to his riches in glory in Christ Jesus. Phillippians 4:19. Turn your lack into a seed of what you desire from God.

Delight your self in him and he will give you the desires of your heart. Psalm 37:4 If you only have one seed, sow it. For one seed planted in good ground with faith in God can be multiplied a thousand times.

The Lord God of your fathers make you a thousand times so many more as ye are and bless your as he hath promised. Deuteronomy 1:11

If you are lacking a "joy" seed because of the distractions of life which may cause you to just sow tears. Be encouraged **"They that sow in tears shall reap joy." Psalm 126:5.**

What about health or the lack there of? Sow faith in Jesus' stripes. **"...with his stripes we are healed." Isaiah 53:5.**

What about my heartache, lonliness? Sow trust **that God will never leave you nor forsake.**

What about my sin? Sow belief that ***God is a just God and there is no condemnation to those who are in Christ Jesus. Romans 5:1***

Sow the word in your heart for it will grow strong within you and increase faith. ***The sower soweth the word. Mark 4:14***

The Lord is nigh unto all them that call upon him, to all that call upon him in truth. He will fulfil the desire of them that fear him; he also will hear their cry and will save them. Psalm 145:18-19.

Margaret A. Donaldson Cobb

I Thought it was An Absolute Contradiction

Use these pages to write your version of what you may have thought was an absolute contradiction as it relates to this chapter. Think about after reading this chapter how you would talk with someone about the chapter topic.

Margaret A. Donaldson Cobb

CHAPTER 10: A CHILD CAN LEAD

*T**each the children so they can lead. Train them up, prepare them to take over, talk to them about how to do it. We have to be good leaders so the ones who are following us can continue the legacy that we started for them. And who cares if they exceed or pass us up. That's the result of good training. Let the children lead! I know you think that is a for real* **ABSOLUTE CONTRADICTION.**

The future leaders of the world are our children. What about the children? In the fast-paced society of the 21st century it seems like we are not taking time to raise the children. Is anyone taking time to walk with them, talk with them, teach them wisdom, pass on knowledge, so they can withstand the test of times. Can we slow down and really talk with them? We are so busy trying to make sure that our children have the latest name brand clothing, that they may think contributes to their self worth and yours too. And because of this, we are not teaching them how much debt we're in trying to keep up with the Jones's and the generations to come are not going to do better than us, because we have not taught them what it takes to get to where we are.

Then there are the children having children who are not fully raised, developed, and taught themselves, and they now have a little person they are responsible for raising. How can they teach their children if they have not been taught? Children are being raised without correction, discipline, no respect of

adult leadership. And now we have another generation that may grow up the same way and the cycle continues.
Have you ever taken the time to read Proverbs 30:11-13? It says,

> *11: There is a generation that will curse their father and does not bless their mother.*
>
> *12: There is generation that are pure in their own eyes yet is not washed from their filthiness.*
>
> *13: There is a generation whose teeth are as swords and their jaw teeth as knives to devour the poor and needy for among men.*

Proverbs 22:15 says, *"Foolishness is bound in the heart of a child; but the rod of correction shall drive it far from him."* <u>And her.</u>

I am a firm believer of teaching children, morals, principles, building self esteem, courage to go out faced this world head on. **Teaching them, the earth is the Lord's and the fullness there in and they that live in it.** (Psalm 24:1) Teach them who God really is and that there is a standard to live by. The Bible also says, to get wisdom. And when we're getting this thing call wisdom, make sure you understand it. Things are fine. But things won't save us when the storms of life roll. I like what it says in Isaiah 33:6 …. "Wisdom and knowledge shall be the stability of the time."

Proverbs 1:8 gives wisdom in saying, "My son, (and daughters too) hear the instruction of thy father and forsake not the law of thy mother." This means they may have to listen to your teaching. One of the commandments is for children to honor us, but we have to honor them by raising them with spirituality, morality, integrity, and with discipline. We can no longer allow the world, talk shows, videos to raise our children. The children are our future. Doctors, lawyers, teachers, preachers, all kinds of potential leaders are going to school every day, but if they are not challenged, they won't know. And then we blame them. That's just not right. We are just as responsible for the future and quality of their lives as they are.

Teach them with diligence. They may act like they don't want to listen, but who is the parent? You're driving to a ball game, cut off the radio and take off their headsets. Break the noise and the silence with what you know will give them something that will stick with them all the days of their lives. Teaching our children what's necessary in that we have the power to save them from destruction. Nobody wants to listen to anybody anymore. Is it because no one wants to take time out and talk anymore? The word in Proverbs 22:6, says to train up a child in the way they should go and when they are old they will not depart. Can you train someone without talking?

The absolute contradiction is that we want our children to be leaders but we and to still lead. Although they will make mistakes, making them only gives them knowledge on what to do the next time around. Experience is the best teacher. So let them cook Thanksgiving dinner. Teach them your recipes. Let them babysit. It may teach them another lesson, (abstinence) Let them teach the Sunday school class. Let them say the prayer. Let them, let them, let them.

Another example of an absolute contradiction for adults is, if we let them; *a child can lead.* Which is the title of this chapter. In the Old Testament, we learn that the young were trained to lead. Kings taught their sons in such a way that they would take over their thrones in case of death, regardless of their age.

It would profit this world to train up our children in such away that when it's time for us to retire, cross Jordan whether timely or untimely our children can go on. The truth of the matter is, they are our future leaders of the world.

Train them early to be leaders. If by chance the "trained" decides to go in the opposite direction; at least you did your part. Teach them to trust, fear, praise and lean on God. "When they grow old, they will not depart." The result of training them children early.

I believe in the power of prayer. I believe what you speak over your children will come to pass whether good or bad. Deuteronomy 30 gives us a choice of life or death. It also encourages us to choose life. I want us as adults to start speaking life, speaking that which is good over the children. Words have power. Though Mary was young, and Elizabeth was old, they were pregnant with leaders that changed the world. Can we think of our children in a way that they were born to make a difference in this cold world? Can we see them teaching, preaching, healing bodies, inventing products that will cure diseases, being good presidents - whether in business or the United States? Strong businessmen and women. A major future leader of this world? Operating in honesty, integrity, and boldness. Humble, proclaiming if it had not been for the Lord being on their side, they would be nothing.

Even if your child may be in a situation where they are incarcerated, teenage parents, strung out on drugs, etc..... can you still speak life over them? Your answer should be

YES! Can you still pray, be a priest and protect them even when they have hurt you the most? Your answer should be YES!

Luke 1: 42 And she spake out with a loud voice and said, "Blessed art thou among women and blessed is the FRUIT of thy womb. And for women who may have not conceived but long to have a child you too are blessed, if you have fostered or adopted.

Isaiah 65:23 They shall not labor in vain, nor bring forth for trouble; for they are the seed of the blessed of the Lord and their off springs with them.

Ezekiel 38:7 Be thou prepared and prepare for thyself and thou, and all thy company that are assembled unto thee and be thou a guard unto them

God's grace and mercy endures through all generations. Are you raising a future leader for this world and the Kingdom?

Margaret A. Donaldson Cobb

I Thought it was An Absolute Contradiction

Use these pages to write your version of what you may have thought was an absolute contradiction as it relates to this chapter. Think about after reading this chapter how you would talk with someone about the chapter topic.

Margaret A. Donaldson Cobb

CHAPTER 11: SEARCH FOR THE LIGHT IN THE DARK AND LISTEN FOR GOD IN THE MIDST OF THE NOISE

Circumstances are platforms for possibilities to praise God, but sometimes it's dark in the circumstance, so dark that if you just saw a speck of light you might have hope. Kids running through the house, the telephone is ringing off the hook. You can't get away from the stress of life, your job maybe two jobs, bills needing to be paid - children clowning in school, co-workers distracting you, the people are arguing downstairs and next door. Someone's music is so loud you can hear it in your house. And all you want is for it to be quiet. Just a little quiet time to hear what thus saith the Lord in the midst of what looks like confusion.

The Bible said when the ninth plague fell in Egypt, it was so dark, that they could feel it. It was so dark that there was not a speck of light for three days. Exodus 10:21-23 I heard a pastor on the radio say, "there are times when the darkness falls, you may not be able to trace God's hand, but you have to trust his heart." I agree totally. There maybe times when you cannot see God because your circumstance is so dark, that even when you can't see him, you have to do your best to believe, He is there. There have been times when my situation was that dark and all I felt that all I could do was trust Him. In the same week of hearing the preacher on the radio, there was a major blackout that affected more than 50 million people. The difference with the blackout in New York, to the one in Egypt or people in dark situations was that there was some light that pierced through the darkness. Some places had back up generators, car lights were on and some people seemed not to have taken this too seriously. I saw an interview with a lady who was trapped in an elevator by herself and right next to her she could hear others in another elevator being rescued. And even knowing she was there alone no one came to help her as a matter of fact they told her they were leaving. She was left alone in the dark, with a host of angels giving her strength and a testimony.

I have concluded that when it's the darkest, light has to be on its way. If you have ever had your lights disconnected and had to wait till the next day to get them turned back on, then you can relate to the children of Israel when the Bible said the moved scarcely. You can't move freely in the dark, you may stumble and fall or bump into a wall. This is when being still and knowing that God is God is all you can do. To the unbeliever the absolute contradiction can be that even when you're in a dark place, if you are carrying Jesus with you, then you have all the light you need. The ultimate light of the world, the one who came that if you would choose him, you would have light. He knows about being in the dark, there was a time when the sun refused to shine on him and he felt as though God was not with him.

THE BEGINNING OF DARKNESS

Genesis 1:1-2a *In the beginning God created the heaven and the earth. And the earth was without form and void and darkness was upon the face of the deep. Fast forward.* ***Jeremiah 1:5a*** *Before I formed thee in the belly, I knew thee and before thou camest forth out of the womb I sanctified thee.*

I Thought it was An Absolute Contradiction

I knew you before I placed you in your mother's womb, saith the Lord. The womb is a place on the inside where no one can see in without an ultrasound and you can see out - it's a DARK PLACE. Inside this dark place, you were warm, fed, had plenty of water, enough room to grow and all of your needs were being met. You would be there however long it took the Lord to shape, form and prepare you for the outside. Now if we started in darkness and he brought us out. If we find ourselves in the darkness of life, the same God that delivered us from the beginning of darkness will deliver us again.

When God told Moses before the ninth plague to go to Pharoah, He had told Moses what to expect. Moses knew what the consequences were going to be. He knew that Pharaoh was not going to submit to his authority, he knew that if he did not God was going to launch darkness in such away that everyone would feel it. People would be moving slowly or not at all because the darkness had paralyzed them.

What is the difference between the issues you face and what they faced? Have you not ever been in a situation were it so dark that you could not see your way through? I realized there are some of you who will claim you have never been in a dark place, but I charge them to live a little while longer. There are those who have psychologically blocked the dark moments out of their minds. The boasting of never being in the dark, the refusing to admit they are or have been in the dark or the denial itself about it is all unhealthy.

The boastful and prideful can give the illusion or just think that nothing will ever happen to them. The ones who are not true to themselves, may find themselves in a position of depression because they refuse to let people know how vulnerable they really are by keeping up a false image. The ones who are in denial, may find themselves in their own personal solitary confinement.

God is trying to get us to place where we admit that we need Him to continue working on us and to keep shining his light down on the inside of us. I remember a time when circumstances were overwhelming and situations dark very dark. I would lay down to go to sleep and sometimes when I would close my eyes and see light or may even dream. Well, I closed my eyes and saw nothing but darkness. Tears begin to roll because I felt as thought my little light had been disconnected and the darkness was upon me. So, I began to call on the name of Jesus and it was like glimpses of light broke through the darkness. Like balls of lightning, Jeremiah 33:3 says to call on the name of the Lord and he will show you great and mighty things. Rays of hope.

Those of us who have learned how to lean on Jesus in the dark times have an awesome responsibility to be and show light in this dark world.

LIFE

Life can sometimes seem to be a dark absolute contradiction. It's good in the morning and by nightfall hell opened the doors and now it's bad. Life is full of all things and for some reason all things are supposed to work for good. All includes the bad, so how can this be? Life - if you take the "l" and "e" away you have the word "if". Aren't we always saying if we had this or if we had that thing would be different? Lazarus' sisters cried out to Jesus "if he had been there, their brother would not have(John 11) If you take the "f" away, you have "lie" and can we feel sometimes that life is a great big lie. The truth is that the devil is the liar. But when all the letters come to together, they make "life" and what does God say, He says to, "choose life." So now you want to know where is God when the issues of life are screaming at you? It so dark that you can feel the darkness. What do you do? The Bible says, to lay aside every weight, cast your burdens on him. HOW? You ask. The Bible says to be of good courage even when you are in such turmoil. The Bible says that God cares for you and your response is, "I can't tell". The Bible says, God will supply all of your needs and in the physical you're losing your house, your car, your children are straying away from your teaching. The Bible says, to count it ALL joy and today on your calendar is long suffering. And here is where I thought God's way was an absolute contradiction.

You're trying with all you heart, mind and soul to keep your mind on Him because you heard that He would keep your in perfect peace. You're trying with everything you have to delight yourself sincerely in Him because you know what was promised to you, that you will receive the desires of your heart. You go to bed with the determination that tomorrow is going to be better than yesterday, and today's trials are for today. So, you wake up wanting to put the garment of praised and realize that you fell asleep wearing the garment of heaviness from the day before. The enemy is still whispering in your ear the worse. The bills are still due. The children are still acting crazy. Your spouse may say something opposite of politeness or may add more pressure to your day. And it's 4:00 in the morning. And because of the issues of life, you feel you can't delight yourself in Him because you're in the dark and cannot feel God. And here again is where I thought God's way was an absolute contradiction.

You're trying to figure out if today is the day that all things are going to prove itself to really work for good. You're trying to figure out if you're being heard today because you have cried out to God for His help. You're wanting God to hear your prayers. And this too, is where I thought God's way was an absolute contradiction.

It's so contradictory that we always want God to hear us and respond immediately when we cry out. And because we do not feel or see God working immediately, we may lose faith. We may feel God is not working on our behalf, when in all actuality He is doing just that. Just imagine 4:00 in the morning, right before the dawn it's the darkest, but the sun is planning on rising. He will shed light on your situation if you ask Him.

Isaiah 65:24 says, that even before you ask God has already answered. God says to ask anything in His name and that He will do. (John 14:14) God said, that if you call on his name you shall be saved. (Romans 10:13) God may say more than one thing at the same time you hear, see, and feel the opposite, which may cause you to think that this is an absolute contradiction. And you start all over with your list of yesterday today; and even though you have prayed, discouragement is still at the top of your list.

The fact is that God hears your cry and desires to encourage you that he does but, you keep crying out with the chaos and confusion so loud that you can't hear Him. You're still talking. Now you're telling your story to anyone who will listen.

My Bible tells me that faith comes by hearing. Well, how can you hear if you're constantly talking about what is

I Thought it was An Absolute Contradiction

wrong? The power of life and death is in the tongue and if you keep speaking death then you keep hearing death and you continue to feel death instead of life.

Beloved, God wishes above all thing that you may prosper. (Paraphrased 3rd John 2. These things are temporary. Trouble comes to past not to stay. Think it not strange when trials come your way. Give no place to the devil. See things as they shall be. Above all listen for God in the noise and when it is dark, search for the light.

And though today you woke up at 4:00 in the morning with the trials of yesterday and what you hear is frustration today and all you see is dark tomorrow; rest assure that God is working just for you. Noise is always a distraction and it's always darkest before the dawn. Your only way out of this is to be still and know that God is God. Just stop. Understand that God knows about every one of your trials. You just have to trust that God, the creator of the earth does not faint nor gets weary and if you just wait on him, he will help you to see your way through the darkness.

I Thought it was An Absolute Contradiction

Use these pages to write your version of what you may have thought was an absolute contradiction as it relates to this chapter. Think about after reading this chapter how you would talk with someone about the chapter topic.

Margaret A. Donaldson Cobb

CHAPTER 12: STANDING ON SHAKY GROUND

Today may feel like all hope is gone. Today I may feel like the foundation is being moved right from under me. Today I cried and felt as though I was not being heard. Today my enemy taunts my soul, by proposing with pressure, now where is your God? Today I felt like falling but in the midst of chaos God encouraged me to stand and answer the enemy with boldness. Where is my God you ask? My faith is, He sitting high and looking low. His son, whose name is Jesus, the one whom I believe was sent, is standing on his right-side making intercession for me. He is presenting my circumstance to my Father that he would hear my cry and deliver me from you, my enemy, that I might stand against the wiles of you. The Holy Spirit is comforting me as this situation gets resolved and I am able to stand on shaky ground.

2 Samuel 22:7-8 In my distress I called upon the Lord and cried to my God; and he did hear my voice out of his temple and my cry did enter into his ears. Then the earth shook and trembled; the foundation of heaven moved and shook because he was wroth.

Dennis Kinbrow wrote a book titled, "What Keeps Me Standing?" It is a book of letters he compiled from grandmothers who wrote to encourage their grandchildren and readers to stand even when the feel they can't. My answer to what keeps me standing once upon a time would have been, "I really don't know." But today my answer is Jesus Christ.

What's your answer to that question? What keeps you standing when your foundation is shaking? When have you had to stand, and the ground felt shaky, and your legs felt so weak that you did think you could stand any longer? Did you take a seat or a deep breath and say, "okay I have to stand through this but the only way I can Lord is with your strength." *My sister and friend in Christ Joyce Turner-Rice said it like this, "God tells you to be still, all awhile he is moving the ground under you."*

The absolute contradiction is in the title, standing on shaky ground. When the ground you are literally standing on is moving, God says "be still". When your house may have been burning down and you had to stand and watch it. Or you were standing outside the car after you had an accident that should have been fatal. You may have had to stand over a loved one who was passing on to glory. You may have had to stand and hear the judge give your child a jail sentence. You may have had to stand in front of the coroners to identify someone you loved and then had to stand at the funeral. Standing on shaky ground is truly a contradiction. You may have to stand when someone tried to knock you down. You may have had to stand because you could not sit and deal with the circumstance. You may have had to stand on what you believe and know what the truth is after you had to listen to someone lie on you. These are some examples of standing on shaky ground.

When has there been a time that is not mention that you had to stand when you really wanted to sit down? When has the scripture "stand like a tree by the rivers of water and not be move," been your testimony? There have been days for me when standing was hard.

But God says, "Be steadfast, unmovable, always abounding in the work of the Lord" (Facing the next day.......) 1st Corinthians 15:58

But God says, "Stand still and see the salvation of the Lord" (Like being on an airplane going through turbulence)

But God says, "Be still and Know that I am God."

Ezekiel 17 *Verse 11 - 13 MIGHT STAND*

Moreover, the word of the Lord came unto ME saying: Say now to the rebellious house, Know ye not what these things mean? Tell them; Behold, the king of Babylon is to come to Jerusalem and hath taken the king thereof and the princes thereof and led them with him to Babylon; And hath taken the king's seed and made a covenant with them and taken an oath of him: he hath also taken the mighty of the land: **That the kingdom might be base, that it might not lift itself up, but by keeping of his covenant it might stand.**

The word "might" contradict the possibility of standing or not. "Might" is not an assurance that something will or will not. I feel what completes this fact is having faith in the one who will help you to stand Some days you know you are strong enough to stand and other days you feel too weak to even try to stand. Doubt and faith cannot reside together. Believe in God, who no matter how shaky the ground is God is still there. He created us human who without him would not be able to stand.

Jeremiah 6:16 Thus saith the Lord, stand ye in the ways and see, ask for the old paths, where is the good way and walk therein, and ye shall find rest for your souls.

There are times when we just don't know which way to go. What I have learned in life is whatever you are going through, good, or bad you're going to have to stand and deal with it. I have seen some people lose so much because depression kept them from standing. Depression had them sitting or staying in bed or on the couch. To overcome we must stand even when it feels likes the foundation under us is shaking.

There is a reason why Dennis Kimbrow asked grandmothers to write letters to their grandchildren about what kept them standing. Though it may seem like it's an absolute contradiction, standing on shaky ground just stand. Stand on the promises of God. Stand on the faithfulness of God. Stand on the prayers of your grandmothers. Just stand.

I Thought it was An Absolute Contradiction

Use these pages to write your version of what you may have thought was an absolute contradiction as it relates to this chapter. Think about after reading this chapter how you would talk with someone about the chapter topic.

_____
_____
_____
_____
_____
_____
_____
_____
_____
_____
_____
_____
_____
_____
_____
_____
_____
_____
_____
_____
_____
_____
_____

Margaret A. Donaldson Cobb

CHAPTER 13: A WAY THAT SEEMS RIGHT

Proverbs 14:12 There is a way which seemeth right unto a man, but the end thereof are the ways of death.

Wise men still seek him. Some still doubt him. Others hate him without a cause. Movies have been made about him. Sometimes during the course of your day, you may see "WWJD" People wanting to know, "what would Jesus do?"

Jesus being who he is would obey and do the work of his father. Unfortunately for us is, though we seek to know what he would do, we still don't do it. By doing our own thing we fall short. We find excuses or make up excuses to justify why we think our way is right, even when it opposes what Jesus would do.

Jesus clearly states things we should not do, and we use scriptures as an excuse, such as, "the flesh is weak." (Matthew 26:41)

We tend to justify wrong because of a way that seems right to man. I was talking with my husband about someone whose choice for a mate would be the same as they are. The concern for their happiness was a point, knowing they would not be happy in a relationship the way God had designed it to be. Male and female. If we were two people who did not know the Lord - then we could have justified their alternative lifestyle by just wanting them to be happy. Seems like the sins of the world are just being accepted as right. And calling things out that are wrong, is wrong. But sin is sin and because of sin it separates us from God.

We allow things to happen and allow the world to intimidate the church by using scripture; "judge not lest you be judge." (Matthew 7:7)

A way that seems right is to let anything go just to get along with folks or stack our churches without standards, or our homes all in the name of acceptance and not offending. So now everything is out of control. Do you think this would happen back in the "day"?

I must admit that one of my favorite T.V. shows <u>used</u> to be a show that depicted all manner of sin. I was drawn in by the humor of the show, the personality of the characters until one day God revealed to me, this show is one of the reasons the world is going to hell in a hand basket. It had gay men, one living with a woman who had several types of relationships out of marriage, her best friend was a drunk, looking to marry old dying men with money. And yes, it was funny, I realized that it was wrong. But that's just one example of sin being thrown in our faces, and we accept it because it's called, "entertainment."

My children justified rap music by the beat, but the words were being heard and understood. It is the lyrics to the songs that are poison. Unfortunately, the beat attracted older people/us because the background music was music from our era.

The church is almost as much to blame by looking more like the world, not standing up for Jesus Christ and what we know to be right, ordaining individuals with alternative living, sexual sin, some of the music sounds like a club and some "dance" to it like they were in one. Justifying by dancing for the Lord. Come to church to find a mate and not knowing or feeling they need to repent - all because of "a way that seems right."

Parents allow children to talk to them any kind of way, all in the name of expressing themselves. When only foolishness comes out. Respect is not taught to them from the parents, so therefore, they talk to and disrespect all manner of authority. And we wonder why the children are the way they are.

Some examples of adults aren't good for the children. For some have been abused by them. You take them to a safe place (school, church, the neighbors...) and years later you find out that some one there had abused them - all because some adult felt their way was right.

Proverbs 14:12 There is a way which seemeth right unto a man, but the end thereof are the ways of death.

The absolute contradiction is the word "seem". It only seems wrong is right but it's really not that way. Our ways are contrary to God's ways, because his thoughts are not ours and his ways are not our ways. God is spirit and we are born of flesh.

Galatians 5:16 -17 This I say then, walk in the Spirit, and ye shall not fulfil the lust of the flesh. For the flesh lusteth against the Spirit, and the Spirit against the flesh; and these are _contrary_ the one to another: so that ye cannot do the things that ye would.

We are all responsible for our actions. What we do, say, how we treat people, taking forgiveness for granted. We hide behind God knows our hearts, God will forgive but we may still have to deal with the consequences. We have let one- or two-people's thoughts change our minds or and have created an overwhelming sense of entitlement.

God will forgive, but not without us paying a price first. The cost of committed sin is too high of a price to pay. Is it worth it? The Bible says, "the wages of sin is death". (Romans 6:23)

The ultimate contradiction is where do we go when we die? Heaven, hell or purgatory? Who gets in and who does not? Do you believe there is a Heaven? Do you believe there is a hell? Surely purgatory is not in the lineup. Heaven - everybody wants to go but no one wants to die. Hell - no way there could be of place of tormenting forever, but it is.

Heaven is where God resides - Jesus says he is the only way to get to the Father. John 14:6

It's more than just being a good person. But it is as simple as believing on the one God sent which is his son Jesus Christ. It's more than you have nice things - God says seek his Kingdom first. It's more than having a good job, making lots of money, that provides you with the liberties to do what you please. It's so much more than what we think. Your belief, service, and offerings to God through his son Jesus is the way. And though you may not think that's right - remember _A way of a man **seems** right leads to distruction._

God is so much more than a modern-day Genie that you call on when you want something - get it and then put him back in a bottle. It's your belief, confession that seals your salvation until the day of redemption, that you might have the possibility of forever being saved and living with God in Heaven. Salvation is from God - something you can't lose - regardless of what someone who thinks their way is right. But you have to work out your soul salvation daily.

Proverbs 14:12 There is a way which seems right unto a man, but the end thereof are the ways of death.

Margaret A. Donaldson Cobb

I Thought it was An Absolute Contradiction

Use these pages to write your version of what you may have thought was an absolute contradiction as it relates to this chapter. Think about after reading this chapter how you would talk with someone about the chapter topic.

Margaret A. Donaldson Cobb

CHAPTER 14: FORFEITED PEACE/NEEDLESS PAIN

"Oh what peace we often forfeit, oh what needless pains we bear, <u>all</u> because we do not carry everything to God in prayer". (What A Friend we Have in Jesus by Joseph M. Scrivens, 1855) What I have learned, is that you cannot walk through it without praying. This random or daily act of faith may contradict some who may have obtained everything from breath to death without praying. But remember the name of the book is "I Thought it was An Absolute Contradiction".

Prayer is not to be taken lightly, made mockery of or do because you want something from God. God sent his son Jesus to live as an example, to be crucified to show forgiveness and to die that we might live. He came as our savior. He is the ultimate prayer warrior. He is a pray<u>er</u> and a prayer answerer. Isn't that ironic? One who prays also answers prayer. It like a teacher. One who teaches also learns. Prayer is so much more than a request to obtain wealth, health, for personal gain. It is the believers of Christ way to commune with God.

Prayer is an act of faith. There are people who may not go to church but understand prayer. They may read a book about prayer and apply it to their lives. Then there may be believers who may not exercise the power of prayer for their lives. Some people may feel they are not worthy of what they would like to ask God for; they dismiss, "ask anything in my name that I will do" saith the Lord. But what do I call that? What else? An Absolute Contradiction.

All IN HIS HANDS

All includes the good, the bad, the pretty and the ugly. Everything is in this three-letter word - nothing is left out.

All in Romans 6:23 says, "*All* have sinned and fallen short of the glory of God. Sin separates us from God. It is not in the minimum or magnitude of the sin, because *all* sin is sin. The first part of Romans 5:8 says "The wage of sin is death." And that's true. It's not always a physical death but death can affect our peace, our freedom, our coming out and going in. The purpose of the cross was that Jesus who knew of no sin, would take on our sins to save us from sin, praying for us to the point of blood, sweat and tears in the Garden of Gethsemane prior to his demise. Which gives merit to the second part of Romans 5:8 "the gift of God is eternal life." The two thieves on crosses with Jesus sins were so great that their punishment would be death by the cross as well. One was so remorseful recognizing Jesus to be one of holiness asked / prayed at that time for forgiveness, became a new creature, obtained grace, mercy and favor, and resides in paradise forever. At that time, he forfeited suffering forever and gained life and peace eternally.

Yes, *all* have sinned. But when we accept Christ, put it *all* in his hands - he is such a just God to forgive and continues to pray for us. This does not give us card blanche to just sin and do what we want to - NO - lest we take God and Jesus for granted. There will be consequences. We can be haughty, arrogant, non-repentive or we can sincerely pray and ask for forgiveness and be shown grace and mercy.

And you being dead in your sins and the uncircumcision of your flesh, hath he quickened together with him having forgiven you *all* trespasses. Blotting out the handwriting of ordinances that was against us, which was contrary to us and took it out of the way, nailing it to the cross. *Colossian 2: 13 - 14*

Placing *all* things in God's hands is the best thing we can do for ourselves.
We do that with prayer. When we fail, when we see ourselves losing or looking like we are losing, when we are sick, and it looks like we're not going to get well, when we have lost children, parents, friends even an enemy, we must pray. When tragedy happens to others we may not know, still we must pray. When we you worked years and right before retirement, the company fires you. When you have been loyal to people, and they did not return loyalty. When we have lied or been lied on. When the perfect storm hits. A perfect storm is when *all* elements of the universe are coming at you on every side. The billows seem not to want to cease, and you can barely stand. I suggest you pray and then stand. And when you have done *all* you can, when you think you have no more power to stand, pray to God that he will keep you standing through it *all*. Build your hope on nothing less that Jesus Christ and his righteousness. Faith in prayer can give you peace during it *all*.

What's the absolute contradiction? Receiving and believing hope, faith and peace in the midst of a perfect storm without wavering, without asking God why, how or when will it end? You know you're going to ask. See God has promised to never leave us nor forsake us. When Jesus ascended up to Heaven, he said, this peace I leave with you, the world didn't give, and the world can't take it away. He promised not to leave us comfortless for the holy spirit would be with us. He will supply ***all*** that we need and instructs us not to be anxious for anything, but for everything ask in prayer and supplication. And it ***all*** will be given according to his riches and glory.

Remember, what the devil means for evil, in God's hands, it is meant for good.

The absolute contradiction to those who don't believe is that the Bible says and it's true, "***All*** things work together for good to them that love the Lord and are called according to this purpose. *Romans 8:28*

IS YOUR *All* ON THE ALTAR? It would behoove you to leave it there.

PEACE AFTER PRAYER

"There is therefore now no condemnation to them which are in Christ Jesus who walk not after the flesh, but the spirit". *Romans 8:1*
"For God sent not his son into the world to condemn the world; but that the world through him might be saved". *John 3:17*

These things have I written unto you that believe on the name of the Son of God; that ye may Know that ye have eternal life and that ye may believe on the name of the Son of God. And this is the confidence that we have in him, that, if we ask anything according to his will, he heareth us. And if we know that he hears us, whatsoever we ask, we know that we have the petitions that we desired of him. *1ˢᵗ John 5:13 -15*

(The) Lord hear thee in the day of trouble; the name of the God of Jacob defends thee.

Send thee help from the sanctuary and strengthen thee out of Zion.

Remember all thy offerings and accept thy burnt sacrifice.

Grant thee according to thine own heart and fulfil **all** thy counsel.

We will rejoice in thy salvation, and in the name of our God we will set up our banners; the Lord fulfil **all** thy petitions. Now know I that the Lord saveth his anointed; he will hear him from his holy heaven with the saving strength of his right hand. *Psalms 20: 1 - 5*

Now unto him that is able to keep you (and me) from falling and to present you (and me) faultless before the presence of his glory with exceeding joy. To the only wise God our savior, be glory, and majesty, dominion, and power, both now and ever. AMEN *Jude 1:24 -25*

Margaret A. Donaldson Cobb

I Thought it was An Absolute Contradiction

Use these pages to write your version of what you may have thought was an absolute contradiction as it relates to this chapter. Think about after reading this chapter how you would talk with someone about the chapter topic.

Margaret A. Donaldson Cobb

Born to Die / Died that I might live.

CHAPTER 15: I THOUGHT IT WAS AN ABSOLUTE CONTRADICTION

In the beginning God created the Heavens and the Earth
Genesis 1:1 KJV

And God said, <u>Let us</u> make man in our image, after <u>our</u> likeness...
Genesis 1:26a KJV

In the beginning was the Word and the Word was with God and the Word was God. The same was in the beginning with God. All things were made by him and without him was not anything made that was made. In him was life and the life was the light of men. And the light shineth in darkness and the darkness comprehended it not. There was a man sent from God whose name was John. The same came for a witness to bear witness of the Light, that all men through him might believe. He was not that Light, but was sent to bear witness of that Light. That was the true Light, which lighteth every man that cometh into the world. He was in the world and the world was made by him and the world knew him not. He came unto his own and his own received him not. But as many as received him, to them gave he power that believe on his name.
John 1:1-12 KJV

God that made the world and all things therein, seeing that he is Lord of Heaven and earth, dwelleth not in temples made with hands. Neither worshiped with men's hands, as though he needed any thing, seeing he giveth to all life, and breath, and all things. And hath made of one blood all nations of men for to dwell on all the face of the earth, and hath determined the times before appointed and the bounds their habitation. Acts 17:24 -26

The Prophets prophesied about him. Others declared not to close their eyes until the day they laid eyes on the one that God would send. Some taught about him and some learned from him. His own did not believe He was the Savior and till this day they still reject him. Others bowed down and received him unto themselves. Others are just clueless as to who He is. Some call on him because they believe, others feel because the word says they will receive abundant life; they think that means abundant in things.

He was born of a virgin. His earthly father was a carpenter. He was teaching in the temple at twelve years old. He chose twelve men to walk with him daily. His mother had faith in who he was. He performed miracles. Cleaned his father's house. He taught folks by night. He fed, healed and delivered people. He cast out demons, gave sight to the blind, strength to the weak.

You may call Him, El Shaddai, because he is with you. Jehovah Jireh because he is provider, Jehovah Shalom, because he is your peace. Jehovah Nissi because he will fight your battles. Jehovah Rophe is your healer. Jehovah Tsidkenu your righteousness. Jehovah Shammah, the ever present one. Jehovah Rohi, the good shephard. And there are many names for Him. But in the middle of the night, when you can't remember the other names, if you call Him

I Thought it was An Absolute Contradiction

what his Father calls Him, you will call him Jesus. At the name of Jesus demons tremble, the devil flees, the lame walks, blind sees, the hungry are fed. At the name of Jesus, every knee will have to bow, and every tongue will have to confess that He is Lord. The trees and the wind obey him. Smart men fear Him. Wise men still seek Him.

What's the absolute contradiction you ask?
The absolute contradiction is, He came into this world for all people and the people knew him not and hated him without a cause. They saw his miracles with their own eyes, could touch him with their bare hands, rejected him and while they were still non-believers, he laid down his life that they would live. No one took his life; he gave it freely knowing that when they lifted Him up all would be drawn to him.

JESUS

Jesus is too much to put in one chapter. There is no searching to his understanding. He is an absolute contradiction in his own way to them who don't believe.

> You hate - He loves.
> You abuse - He forgives.
>
> You lie - He is honest.
> You take - He gives.
> You ask - He answers.
> You're sick - He heals.
> HE DIED THAT WE MIGHT LIVE.

He was Hezekiah's extension of life.
His desire is that all men, even the ones who hate him, would come to him and be saved.
When placed on an old, rugged tree in the shape of a cross by those who did hate Him - He asked God to forgive them.
When others rejected the children, He bid them to come to Him.
His entire purpose was to be the propitiation, a substitute for our sins that through him we would be forgiven.
He will judge the quick and the dead.
He had a unusual beginning - an absolute contradiction to the design of conception.
He is an intercessor for us. The Father looks at us through His blood and delivers us from all our trials.
A bridge between sin and salvation.
A rejected corner stone but was used to be the chief corner stone.
An innocent man who was found guilty.
The pain of the stripes on his back, will heal the pain in ours. His pain our gain.
The ultimate promise keeper.

Wherefore seeing we also are compassed about with so great a cloud of witnesses, let us lay aside every weight, and the sin which doth so easily beset us and let us run with patience the race that is set before us. Looking unto Jesus the author and finisher of our faith who for the joy that was set before Him **_endured the cross_**, despising the shame and is set down at the right hand of God. For consider Him that **_endured_** such a **_CONTRADICTION_** of sinners against himself, lest ye be wearied and faint in your minds. Ye have not yet resisted unto blood - striving against sin. Hebrew 12: 1-4

He was Born to Die and He Died that we might born again.

I THOUGHT IT WAS AN ABSOLUTE CONTRADICTION

Margaret A. Donaldson Cobb

ABOUT THE AUTHOR

I began writing *I thought it was An Absolute Contradicition* in 2003. Yes, 20 years ago God gave me this title as I was sitting in Dr. Preston T. Adams' III Sunday school class. I cannot remember what was being taught, I just remember my response was "that's an absolute contradiction". Fast forward 20 years since that time the chapter titles have become reality whereas at first, I was writing for encouragement and enjoyment, I now have lived, and I am living each one.

What do you mean by that? Well, the title "Joy in the Midst of Sorrow", was something I would say to encourage others who had suffered loss and now I have. The pain of losing a loved one can be excruciating and the thought of any type of joy contradicted my soul. Losing my husband after 36 years, 13 days, 13 hours - two weeks from our 37th wedding anniversary in 2016, was the hardest thing that had ever happened to me. I cried and cried and the times I did allow joy and laughter, afterwards I felt guilty.

I relate to each chapter personally and pray that this book will give insight into to your lives as you read and use the note pages to create your thoughts of what may seem or have seemed like contradictions in your life.
I/we have raised three awesome adults Andrew, Anthony, and Anita, who could write their own stories of Absolute Contradictions.

My prayer for this book is to reach people where they are in this world of many contradictions. It may be difficult sometimes making decisions that honors God, and it is contrary to what friends, and family may do, and you may find yourself second guessing your decision. This book sheds light on just that, ways that seem right to us may lead to heartache and pain, whereas if we choose God's ways, we can trust that every little thing will work out alright. Even though one may challenge us about God's ways – just know and trust he is the hurt and the healer. And you thought it was too, An Absolute Contradiction.

Who is this book for?

I thought it was an Absolute Contradiction is for everyone. Easy answer. Everyone may not read it. Though having everyone in mine, I hope this book gets in the hands of new Christians, babes in Christ who are trying to understand the basics of who God is and how his ways are not ours.

It can be difficult these days where wrong looks and feels right. Even Politicians are legislating things that once were considered wrong and immoral to be right just to fit a friend or family member's lifestyle that they may not want to offend their ways of thinking. But did anyone check in with God. What does God say? God has the final say. People may not want to hear what God has to say on difficult subject matters. We want God to always be loving and forgiving even though we may not be. And there are people who may not understand things and ask how could and loving God allow bad things to happen. I have asked the same questions and my trust in God and crying out to God kept me standing and gave me comfort. Did that happen right away? Of course not, did I feel it was a contradiction? Of course, I did; but I trusted God through it all.

I Thought it was An Absolute Contradiction will in no way contradict the word of God. The witness in this book will go forth in a way that will cause examination and not judgement. It will be simple but profound. Encouraging and inspirational. Prayerfully enjoyed by all who will read it. Unfortunately, those who may really need this book may never read it; but you will and if ever you get the chance to share it let him or her know that the sacrifice and love of God was not / is not An Absolute Contradiction.

I Thought it was An Absolute Contradiction

Margaret A. Donaldson Cobb

Enhanced DNA Publishing
www.EnhancedDNAPublishing.com
info@EnhancedDNA1.com
317-537-1438

www.ingramcontent.com/pod-product-compliance
Lightning Source LLC
Chambersburg PA
CBHW050645160426
43194CB00010B/1812